photographing
babies & toddlers

photographing
babies & toddlers

JOHN HEDGECOE

COLLINS & BROWN

First published in Great Britain in 2002 by
Collins & Brown Limited an imprint of
Chrysalis Books
64 Brewery Road
London N4
A member of Chrysalis Books plc

Distributed in the United States and Canada by
Sterling Publishing Co., 387 Park Avenue South,
New York, NY 10016, USA

10 9 8 7 6 5 4 3 2 1

British Library Cataloguing-in-Publication Data:
A catalogue record for this book is available from the British Library.

ISBN 1-85585-999-8

Contributing Editor: Chris George
Editorial Director: Roger Bristow
Design Manager: Liz Wiffen
Design: Roger Daniels, Duncan Brown
Picture Coordinator: Jenny Hogg

Reproduction by Classicscan Pte Ltd, Singapore
Printed and bound in Singapore by Craft Print International Ltd

The author would like to thank the following

for their help in producing this book:

Kathleen Hedgecoe, Hayley, Gavin and Megan

Richardson-Gunn, Pentax Cameras, Olympus

Cameras, Agfa Films (all pictures were taken on

Agfa RSX 50, 100 and 200 ISO), Colorama

Photodisplay Limited, Pegasus Pushchairs Limited,

Mexico Tourist Board and all the young models who

were so patient and fun to photograph!

Contents

Introduction

hildren have been one of the most popular subjects for the camera since the invention of photography itself. By the 1850s, every town had its own photographer, whilst itinerant cameramen travelled the villages offering to take portraits of men, women, children and babies. Everyday folk could, for the very first time, have their image perpetuated, and family pictures were no longer just for the rich, famous and aristocratic.

It was the arrival of roll film, and Kodak's promise that 'You press the button, we do the rest', that brought cameras into wider ownership at the end of the nineteenth century.

Despite the convenience, however, photography was still too expensive for most people to do themselves. Portrait studios therefore thrived, and these were the places that you would go to if you a wanted a picture taken of a new addition to the family.

The picture shown opposite is typical of the type of portrait taken of babies during the Victorian and Edwardian eras, taken from my family archive. Such sepia prints could be found framed in most people's houses. The naked poses were not thought unusual, although such pictures would cause much embarrassment for the subjects themselves when they reached their teenage years!

Nowadays, photography is as much a part of bringing up a child as nappy changing and bedtime stories. Thanks to the arrival of digital photography, taking pictures is even more affordable than ever. It would be unusual in many families, in fact, not to start taking pictures from the very first day of a child's life.

In their first two years, children change more rapidly than they do at any other point in their lives. During this period, they develop and achieve new skills at such a rate that you really need to take pictures of them at least once a week — otherwise a stage in their life has gone forever. Without a photographic record, even the parents will find it hard to keep track of just how much they have achieved, and have changed, in such a short space of time.

To photograph the baby in your family you therefore need to be disciplined. You need to develop a schedule, so that you get into the habit of taking regular photographs. Don't just be content with formal pictures that celebrate birthdays and special occasions — your pictures should become a visual diary showing all of a child's moods, achievements and foibles.

Your family album will not just show a baby growing up, it will show places, things and people that were integral to your family's life at the time. It will be a sociological record. So when you, your child, or their children, look back at these photographs in 20 or 50 years time the shots will serve as an aide-memoire to the way things used to be.

Cameras continue to get easier to use, and more 'intelligent'. However foolproof the equipment, though, the fundamental techniques for taking pictures remain the same, whether you use film or digital technology. The photographer still has to decide the camera angle to use, changing zoom setting, background and lens height to suit the circumstance. Even with the perfect composition you must elicit the right expressions. This book will help you to understand the approaches you can use, and the techniques you can try, so that you can be as proud of the portraits you take as you are of the children themselves.

If you'd like portraits of

your babies that are good

enough to hang proudly

on your walls and to give

to relatives, you will

greatly enhance your

chances of success by

following some simple

guidelines. The pictures in

this section show what is

possible, along with 12

fundamental tips to help

you get similar results.

Portfolio

TIP 1
Light work

It is tempting always to use flash when shooting indoors. But you will get better results if you use the light from a nearby window — this will be less harsh and provide more flattering lighting. Move the baby to the best-lit spot in the house.

▶ **FILLING IN THE DETAIL**
It may seem harder to control daylight than flash, but you can still influence its effect. You can pick where to place the baby in the room. You can control the spread and intensity of bright sunlight using blinds, drapes or net curtains. You can also 'bounce' light into unlit areas using a reflector, such as a white sheet. Here, I used a mirror to reflect light into the face.

▶ **ABIGAIL AT 8 MONTHS**
The light for this shot comes from windows behind the baby girl, as well as from both sides. The daylight is soft as the baby sits mainly in the shadows — but this form of lighting can be very pleasing, as it means that the face is uniformly lit.

▶**ELENOR, AGED 3**
In a pose that is
reminiscent of that
of an old oil painting,
this young girl looks
dwarfed by her pony.

TIP 2

Sense of scale

Kids grow fast, and it can be hard to tell a child's age from a photograph, because there is often nothing to indicate their size. Occasionally, it is worth including a scale object in a shot which you can measure the child against in years to come.

▶**OLIVIA AND HOLLY**
In this shot it is a much smaller Shetland pony that provides the sense of scale for the picture. The girl on the left again appears small standing next to this miniature horse, but the girl in the saddle appears oversized for her mount.

TIP 3

Get down!

For the most natural-looking shots of babies, it is important to get the camera down to their level. Depending on their age and what they are doing, this might mean lying or kneeling on the ground so that the lens is level with their eyes.

▼ **MOLLY**
If you shoot pictures of children from head height, you will normally be looking down on the child. For a more flattering view, you should get the camera down to their level. For this shot, I sat on the grass so to get a more natural-looking low-level shot.

▶ **ON THE LEVEL**
Another shot of Molly — but this time with an even more luxurious mode of transport! For this set-up I had the camera on a tripod, so that the car was framed symmetrically and I could concentrate on getting the right pose. The height of the tripod platform, however, was adjusted so that it was at the same height as the child's head.

▶**ALEXANDER**
Although all sorts of toys will keep a child amused, it is worth trying to find ones that will work well in the picture as well. This toy Mercedes Sports fits the bill perfectly. Remember that such props do not have to be bought; they could be borrowed for the day from friends.

TIP 4
Boys' toys!

To keep a young child occupied long enough to get a variety of poses, you need something to distract them. Find photogenic toys for them to play with that will not only keep them amused, but that will also make a handy prop for the portrait.

▶**BARNABUS**
Adventurous toddlers relish the opportunity to climb up onto things. This wooden horse was a perfect prop for a portrait, and it didn't take too much persuading to get the young boy to dress up as a cowboy! Similar shots could be posed on fairground or shopping centre rides.

TIP 5
Lost in space

Most of your pictures should be framed tightly, so that the children fill as much as the picture area as possible. But in some shots it is worth including more of the scene, so that the viewer gets a real idea of just how small the toddler or baby is.

▶ **HOLLY**
By deliberately leaving acres of space around the baby, her small size is exaggerated. She is totally engulfed by the bed. If I had zoomed in more, this sense of scale would have been lost. The secret is to zoom out far enough so that it is obvious that the framing is deliberate, and not just lazy camerawork.

▶ **HOLLY IN TOYLAND**
This is a fun shot that anyone could set up. Completely surrounded by an extensive collection of teddies, dolls and other soft toys, the baby is practically lost from view. If you don't have enough furry animals to hand, you could borrow more from friends.

◄ MEGAN, 10 DAYS OLD
A car safety seat makes an ideal place in which to pose a newborn baby, as he or she can sit undisturbed without risk of coming to harm. Here the seat is covered with a white blanket, so that the baby stands out better in a room full of congratulatory cards and flowers.

► MEGAN AT 2 MONTHS
Even before a baby's neck and back have developed sufficiently to enable them to sit up on his or her own, he or she can be propped up in all manner of chairs — making him or her appear quite regal in a suitably soft seat or sofa. Babies may topple at any second, however, and it is essential that someone is waiting just out of shot to support the baby should he or she begin to keel over.

TIP 6
Take a seat

Babies can not sit up on their own for the first few months, but from a few days old they can be propped carefully on a chair. Such shots are fun, as they make babies look older than they actually are.

TIP 7
Kith and kin

▼ TEGAN, TAMZIN AND JORJA
Older sisters and brothers will love posing proudly with the new addition (or additions) to the family. Here, the addition of the sister to the composition not only creates a valuable shot for the album, but she can also ensure that the twins do not topple over.

With a baby in the house, it is easy for other photographic subjects to be forgotten. But do regularly shoot babies with other family members, young and old. These shots will be especially poignant to the baby when he or she grows up.

▶ TEGAN AND TAMZIN
Not everyone gets twins in the family — but this does not mean that you cannot photograph two or more babies at the same time. In fact, new mothers usually meet, and make friends, with other women with similarly aged babies. These babies then grow up as friends, and it is nice to capture early shots of them together, at sleep or play.

TIP 8
Clearing clutter

Cluttered backgrounds don't usually work with portraits. Sometimes you can throw distracting things behind the subject out of focus. But it pays to look out for suitable places to pose your subject where the background is either plain or complementary to the subject matter, rather than working against it.

▶ **SARAH**
Once you have found a successful backdrop or setting for a picture, it is worth making the best use of it that you can. This means not only shooting lots of pictures but also re-using the set-up to photograph others. Here, the fireplace gets a second chance to be used as a 'frame within a frame', this time framing Ella's younger sister.

▶ **ELLA**
A fireplace might not seem the obvious place in which to pose a child for a portrait, but here the dark tiles and surround create a perfect background for the girl dressed in white. The fireplace creates a frame around the subject that draws the eye in the picture.

TIP 9
Using props

One of the easiest ways to strengthen a portrait is by the careful use of props. A large toy or an interestingly shaped chair can provide instant impact to a shot. Other excellent props for young children include balloons, hats and umbrellas.

▶ **LARA AT 22 MONTHS**
It was the graphic shape of this elaborate cane chair that inspired this shot. Set against a plain tarpaulin backdrop, its curves make a perfect cove for a young child to perform in.

◀ **REGAL POSE**
Thanks to the gold
paint, rich fabric and
architectural hallway
the young girl appears
quite different from the
one opposite, although
in fact it is the same girl,
at the same age.
Enjoying playing the
part of lady of the
manor, Lara was happy
to sit long enough for
several successful shots
to be taken.

TIP 10
Mother's help

It is impossible to concentrate on the camera and child at the same time. To get the baby looking towards the camera and in a good humour, you will need the help of mum or dad, who can coax and comfort the child from just out of shot.

◤**REASSURANCE**
Very young babies need to feel the security of the people they know around them. So for a successful shoot you will need to engage the assistance of someone the baby knows well — and for the very young, this inevitably means mum. Assistants can also be ready to wipe faces and to jump to the rescue should the child begin to topple.

TIP 11
Take advice

The older that children get, the more they will want to play to the camera. By the time they are toddlers, you may find that the best way to get their cooperation for a photo session is to let them suggest locations, clothes, poses and props.

▶ **BETH AND JO**
Often children like to pose with favourite toys — a treasured doll, perhaps, or a pretend mobile phone. Giving them the choice helps make them feel involved. You can always suggest your own set-ups later. These twins were keen to show off their new bikes.

▶ **TRIBAL HEAD-DRESS**
Most children like to put on fancy dress, and getting them to choose something from their dressing-up box for the photo shoot is a good way of getting them to help you to get good poses. Costumes for favourite film and cartoon characters are particularly popular, and can often be hired.

▶ **ELLIOT ON RED CHAIR**
On this driveway, the only possible backgrounds appeared to be the house itself or the street in front. However, rather than getting down to the boy's eyelevel, I stood up as I shot, turning the herringbone pattern of the paving stones in the backdrop for the picture.

TIP 12
View from above

Although it is best to shoot from the child's level (see page 14), clutter in the background may make this impractical. A simple way to manufacture a plainer backdrop is to shoot from high up so the floor, grass or carpet becomes the background.

▶ **ELLIOT IN THE TUB**
Shooting from a standing position gives a bird's-eye view when photographing a child. The horizon or walls disappear, turning what is below your feet into the backdrop. This can sometimes simplify a portrait, although the elevated camera angle should not be overused.

From birth until the first

birthday, a baby changes

beyond recognition. As

the baby grows, he or she

seems to learn new skills

every day. To avoid

missing key milestones,

your camera needs always

to be ready for action.

The pictures in this section

show the progress of one

baby, Megan, over her

first 12 months...

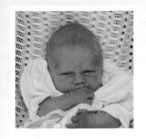

Baby's first year

Day one

◀ ALL IN WHITE
Keep the surroundings in your pictures as simple as possible. Here, the white bed linen, radiator and robe not only create a plain canvas on which to frame mother and child, they create a bright, 'high-key' effect which is particularly flattering for female portraiture.

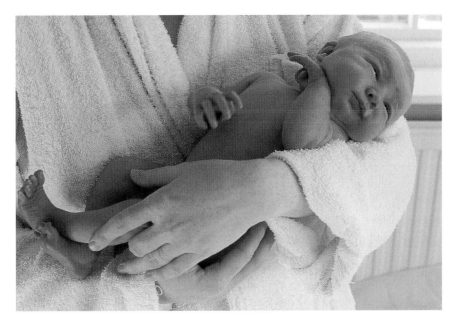

IN MOTHER'S ARMS
Baby Megan on her first day, cradled by her mother, Hayley. This picture was taken without the use of flash, creating a softer, more atmospheric shot than the one opposite. When possible, always shoot some pictures with the flash turned off, even if this means using a faster, grainier film.

NEW NOISES
It is not just the new equipment and baby that have to be got used to — there is the heart-wrenching sound of crying to get accustomed to. Here, Dad experiments with ways to comfort Megan.

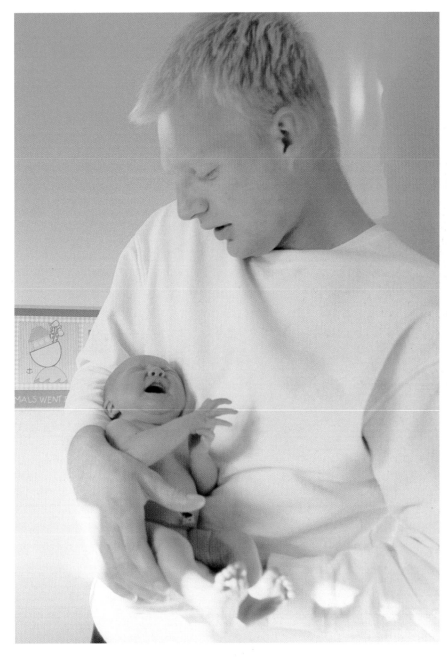

The first few hours after the birth are a joyous, but hectic, time for the newly expanded family. Mother and child try to take some rest from the exertions of labour, whilst getting used to each other. Father spends all his time passing on the news to friends and relations, whilst rushing on errands between home and hospital.

Not surprisingly, in this atmosphere serious photography tends to be forgotten. Snaps of the baby are, of course, taken to show all and sundry, but the tiredness of the subjects and the clinical atmosphere of the maternity ward do little to inspire great pictures.

But this is the beginning of a long journey for the new baby, and these early shots are the essential start for the latest volume of the family album. The child will never be smaller, or look more fragile — he or she will change so fast that you need to take every opportunity you can to take photographs. Inevitably, you will need to be disciplined about your picture-taking if you are to get an unbroken record of the child's early years. And you might as well start by making the effort to take some serious pictures in the hospital itself. This is therefore where my sequence of pictures of baby Megan began.

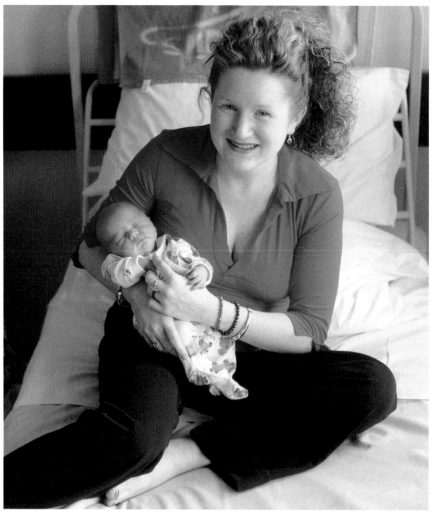

Day two

It might not seem it at the time, but the first few days after the birth are the ideal opportunity for a for a more serious portrait session for a several reasons.

With so much help at hand from nurses and family, the mother has more time on her hands than she will have in the coming weeks. The child is also tired after the exertions of birth, and may therefore be a more cooperative subject than he or she might in a few days time.

Mothers frequently feel down immediately after the birth, and they may well appreciate, with a little coaxing, the chance to do their hair and take time over their make-up so as to look their best for the camera.

◤ GOOD NIGHT'S SLEEP
With the chance of some rest, the mother is likely to be much more amenable to being photographed on the second day.

◀ THE GRIP REFLEX
Even at birth, babies cannot help grasping anything placed in the palm of their hand. This primitive reflex is one of the ways that helps create a bond between parents and baby, and is well worth trying to catch on film.

◄ **ALL THE FAMILY**
A full family portrait when the baby is just a few days old will be a particularly precious picture for years to come. The secret of arranging two or three people in front of the camera is often to sit one behind the other with their heads touching.

Day three

When a baby is born, it might seem that he or she can do very little for him- or herself. But although babies cannot talk, move around or sit up on their own, they have many innate abilities. They can communicate by crying for attention, they can suck to get their food, and they can grip with surprising force. They may wiggle their toes if the soles of their feet are touched, and can often be soothed, though not always, simply by being picked up.

Their hearing may be muffled at first because of liquid in the ear, but after a day or two they

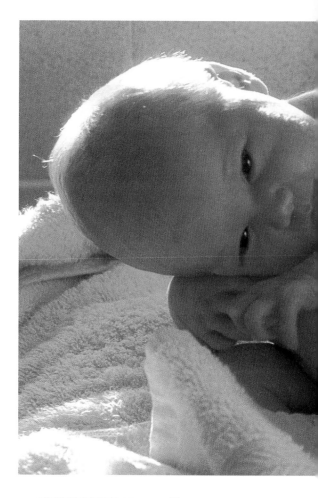

◄ ALL IN MINIATURE
It is the simple things that amaze you about babies. Their hands and feet are perfectly formed , yet so, so tiny. A shot of a limb emerging from a blanket, or a hand shown in close-up in the palm of an adult, will remind you of these things in the months and years to come.

► HAND TO MOUTH
At birth, babies have little control over their hands and arms. However, whenever the hand comes in contact with the mouth, the young child will probably start sucking on the whole fist, as he or she cannot yet separate a single finger or thumb.

◀ **BIG HEAD**
As with all newborn babies, Megan's head looks enormous compared with the rest of her body, and it will be weeks before she can support its weight all on her own. On average, the head is about a third of a baby's total volume at birth.

can hear sounds clearly, and they will respond to loud noises and to voices (female ones in particular). Although they can see, their sight is not well-developed, and they find it very hard to focus on distant objects. However, they like looking at faces if they are close enough (about 25.5cm/10in away) and are fascinated by strong black-and-white patterns and shapes. They will also react to bright lights and see movement.

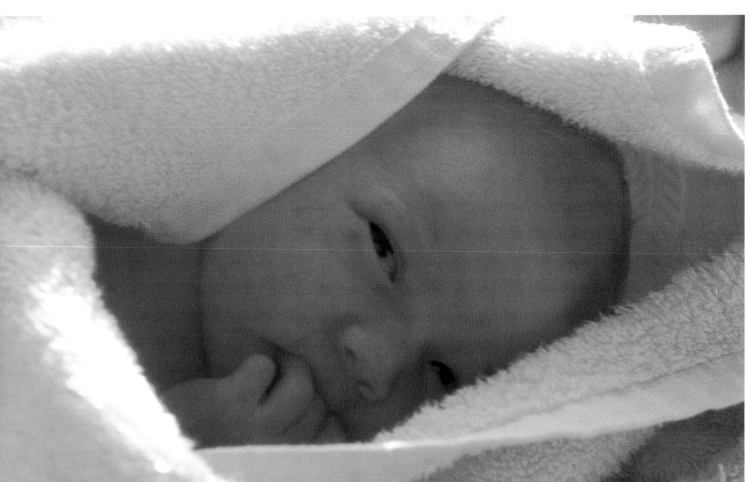

Day four

The arrival of a new baby not only means a new member of the household; it also means finding room for all the paraphernalia that inevitably comes with him or her. Although the child is small, the cots, prams, seats, toys, bottles and so on seem to take over the house. If it is the first baby in the family, the arrival home from hospital signals the start of a completely new way of living.

Although it is tempting to always set up studio type shots, where the baby is shown in isolation and at his or her best, it is always worth taking some shots that show what is going on the background. In five years time, children will be fascinated to see photographic evidence of the soft toys that they were given when they were first born. In ten years time, you will treasure the memories of what the nursery used to look like. In 20 years time, as the parents start thinking about becoming grandparents, it will be fascinating to see the decor, appliances and furnishings that you used to have. Pictures that show how you lived may well bring back feelings and recollections that will be as strong as those stirred by the shots of the baby.

◀ **A DOG'S LIFE**
It is not just the parents that have to get used to the arrival of Megan in the house. The family dog, just visible behind the glass door, tries to work out why it has now been banished from the kitchen.

▶ **PARTIAL VIEW**
Don't forget dad in your early pictures. Notice that only a small part of his face is showing, so that baby Megan can still appear a decent size in the frame. To those who know him, he still remains recognisable.

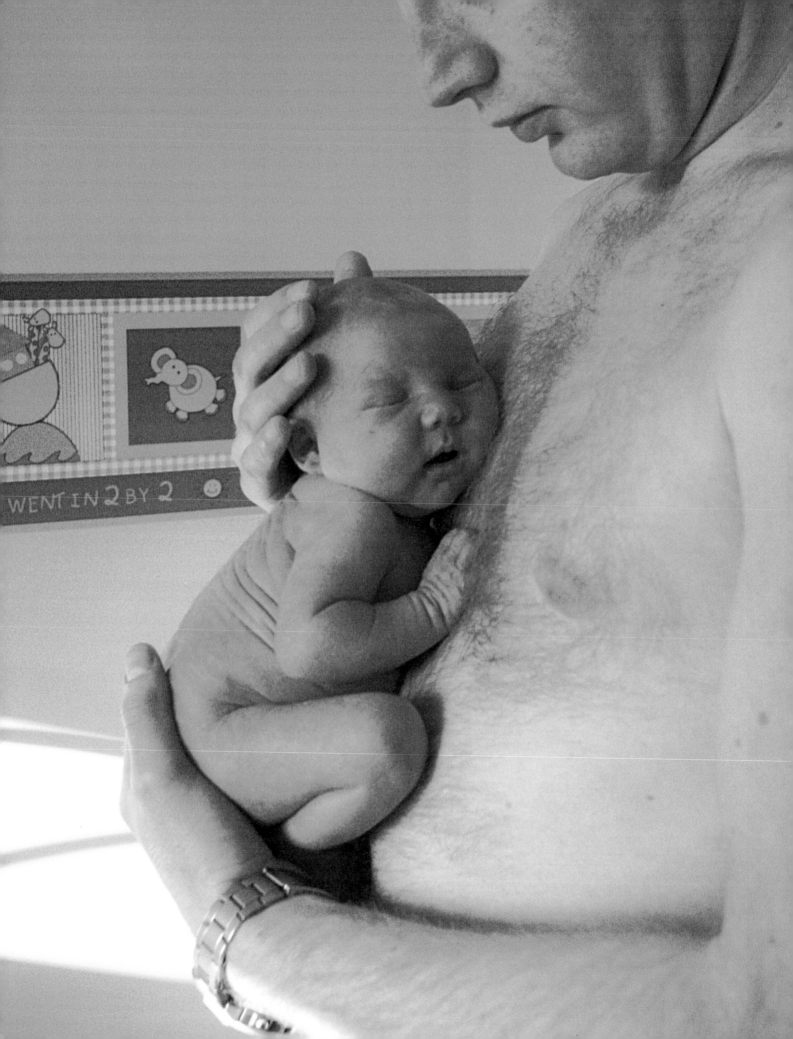

Day ten

As the child heads towards its second week, the young baby and the parents will start to establish some sort of a routine. It will have become pretty obvious that there are three main things that a newborn baby can do well — that is cry, feed and sleep. Although he or she may only sleep for a couple of hours at a time, it is this activity that takes up most of his or her days.

Newborn babes sleep on average for around 16 hours a day. As they will tend to keep everyone busy during their more wakeful moments, this may mean that there is not time during their waking day that is convenient for photography, particularly if parents are going to snatch some sleep.

Fortunately, babies still look beautiful when they are in their slumbers, whether sleeping in a cot, lying on a double bed or pushchair, or in a car seat. You can use these periods — even if they are just catnaps in the middle of the day — in which to catch interesting facial expressions and gestures on film as they sleep.

Remember that at this young age it is still relatively easy to ensure they fall asleep in a better lit, and less cluttered, part of the house.

▶ **MUSICAL CHAIRS**
Megan is quite happy to rest, and fall asleep, in her car seat. This means she can be moved around the room without disturbing her, to make the most of any daylight coming through the windows.

One month

Although babies do not usually smile until they are around six weeks old, it does not mean that they are incapable of showing any emotion before that magical first grin.

Their main weapon is wailing, which is used to mean a multitude of things. It is not easy to tell which means which, but there are certainly different intensities, depending on how hungry they really are, how urgently they need to be changed, or whether they just need to be comforted. This form of early communication is all part of growing up, and although some frown upon photographing a crying baby, this type of shot makes charming studies, which should be captured alongside those more photogenic and formal moments.

◀ ▽ **FULL OF EMOTION**
Megan in one of her more moody moments... The screwed-up face makes such a charming study of typical infant behaviour — even if Megan herself will not be so enthralled with the shots in years to come! On their own, the pictures are interesting enough, but as a sequence, mounted on the same page of an album, they make a much more telling story.

▶ LINE OF SIGHT
By four weeks, Megan's neck muscles are beginning to strengthen, but her head still looks uncomfortable if it is unsupported. Notice how the direction of Hayley's gaze creates an imaginary line that points to the main subject of the picture.

▼ OVER THE SHOULDER
This alternative pose allows both mother and child to look at each other. The camera angle means that Hayley's face is not seen clearly, but this means that the baby becomes a stronger focus for attention. In the movie business, this type of set-up is known as an 'over-the-shoulder' shot.

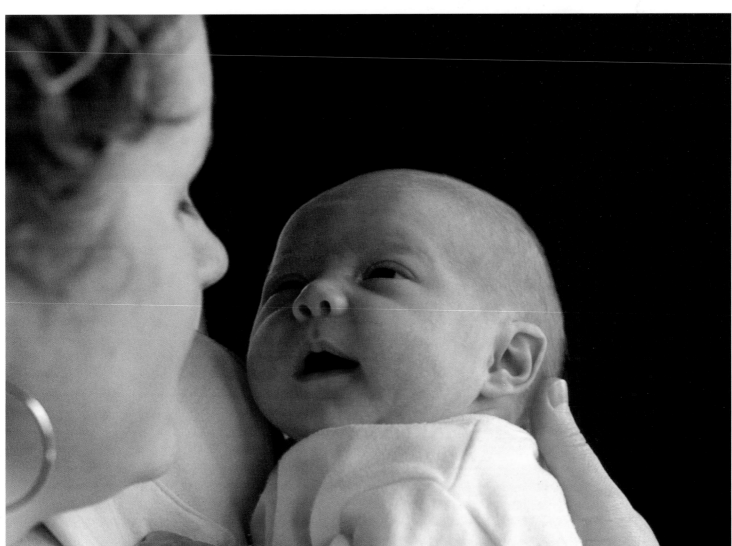

Two months

First smiles are a momentous event for every parent, but they have extra-special significance for the photographer. A happy or contented face is so much more rewarding for the picture-taker. Some argue that early smiles are provoked by wind, but during the second month it will become obvious that smiles are a response to seeing another face.

Smiles, we are told, are an in-built insurance policy, designed to make sure that babies get time and attention from those around them. Early smiles may be given generously to anyone who the baby sees, but gradually he or she becomes more discriminating. By the age of three months, the widest smiles will be reserved for the people that he or she knows and loves the most. As you cannot look at the child and peer through the viewfinder simultaneously, an assistant may be needed to elicit the desired facial responses from your young subject.

▶ **DREAM WORLD**
Nearly half a baby's sleep is spent in the REM (rapid eye movement) state — the part of sleep when we dream. What Megan was dreaming of here, we can only guess.

▽ **FLAT OUT**
During her first few weeks of life, Megan's back has gradually unfurled from its foetal position, and she can now lie more comfortably on her front. Here, the adult's hand not only creates a sense of scale, it also ensures that Megan is both looking in this direction and is smiling.

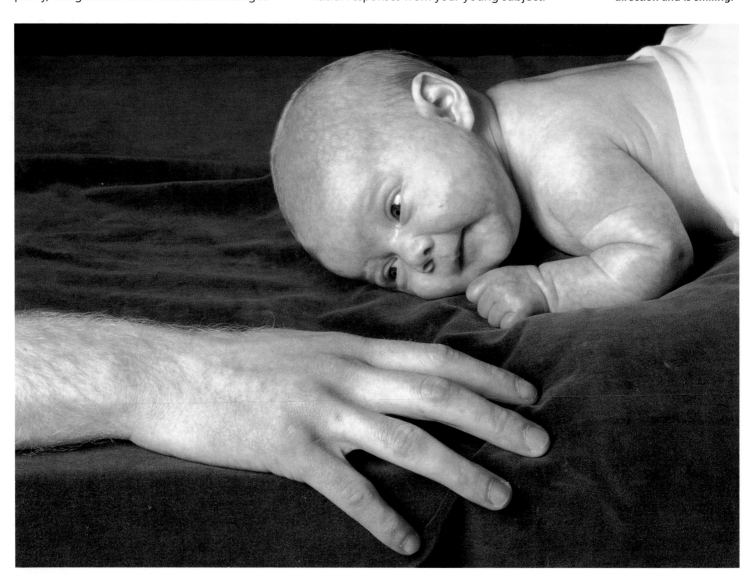

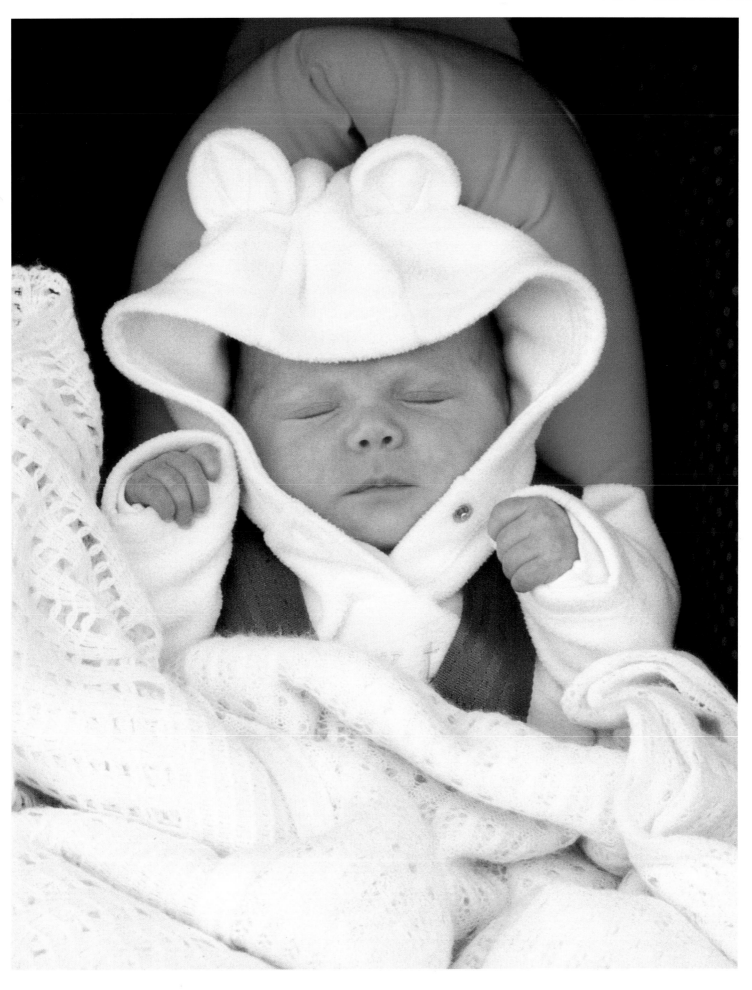

Four months

SPLASH OF COLOUR
Hats are a particularly effective way of adding colour and shape to a baby portrait. In this shot Megan's bright yellow sun hat has helped make this picture look just a little different from others in the album.

B y the time that a baby is four months old, it will have become obvious why people tell you that children grow up fast. The child that was born just 16 weeks ago now looks so very different. The seemingly constant feeding is now really beginning to show, as he or she now weighs roughly double the amount that he or she did when born.

What is more, babies at this age are still continuing to grow at this phenomenal rate. Their height (or more correctly their length, as they cannot yet stand up) has shot up by around a millimetre every day since birth. This might not sound a lot, but his means an average of 2.5cm (1in) growth each and every month.

This constant growth means that the photographer in the family must not let up with his or her picture-taking. Besides, it is from now on that a baby's character really develops...

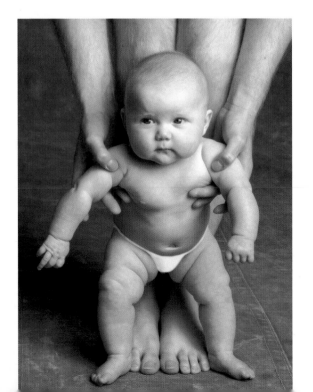

SKIN ON SKIN
The chubby folds of a baby's body become much more visible when they are freed from their outer clothing. But make sure the room is warm, otherwise you will have a bad-tempered baby on your hands.

I CAN SEE YOU!
You don't need a completely clear view of someone's face to make a good portrait. Megan is partly obscured by her mum in this over-the-shoulder shot, but this means that her eyes become an even stronger focal point for the picture.

Six months

There are a number of important milestones in a baby's development that photographers will wish to catch on film. But although you can give an average age when a child starts laughing or crawling, say, every child develops at different rates. Although parents may get anxious, the fact a child achieves things 'late' does not necessarily mean he or she will be less able in the long term; late walkers, for instance, may well be great athletes.

One momentous event that usually occurs around six months is the arrival of the first tooth. This is usually one of the front two teeth on the bottom jaw, and marks the beginning of a two-year long process where the 20 milk teeth will in turn break their way through the child's gums. The discomfort that this periodically causes may on occasion mean that a child is far less well-humoured than usual, and is less cooperative to the photographer.

▼ MAKING FRIENDS
Megan is becoming more aware of other people, recognising those she does and doesn't know. Harvey, a few weeks her senior, has become a regular playmate. Here, the two are enjoying a day out at the park with their mothers. At this age, Megan is also becoming more wary of strangers.

ON THE SLANT
Normally you aim to keep the camera level as possible when taking pictures. However, by deliberately tilting the camera, you can sometimes end up with more interesting compositions, as in this shot. Here, the arrangement creates strong diagonal lines that seem to draw the eye into the picture.

SPACED OUT
A more traditional mother-and-baby pose. Note that without tilting the camera, the two subjects do not fill the frame so well.

Ten months

Between the age of nine months and a year, a baby will learn and then perfect the art of crawling. The new movement brings a new era of independence and adventure to the child's life.

Although many babies will crawl on their hands and feet, a large number use more unconventional means of getting around. They may shuffle on their backsides, for instance, or roll to their chosen destination.

The new stage means that new areas of the home need to be made safe from exploring hands. For the photographer, it may mean that if you want the child to keep in one place for more than a few seconds, you might need to, quite literally, strap them into a chair.

▼ IN THE CHAIR
A high chair provides a perfect way of keeping a baby still and looking in a particular direction, whilst still allowing you to take good close-up portraits. The chair can easily be moved outdoors to get better ambient lighting.

▶ FINGERS AND THUMBS
Megan's hand control is improving all the time, and she has started using her finger and thumb to pick things up. The new-found coordination means she can now suck her thumb far more efficiently.

◀ HAND SIGNALS
At this age, Megan communicates a lot with those around her by waving her hands around and pointing at things. Here she and friend Harvey interact with their mothers, as the photographer catches their facial expressions on film.

Eleven months

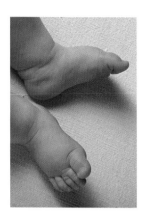

▲ ABSTRACT FIGURE
Extreme close-ups of baby's feet make interesting pictures at any age.

Babies start learning to talk almost from the moment that they are born, but it is unlikely that they will produce more than one or two words before their first birthday. From the cradle, however, babies will make a variety of noises — the baby's first experiments at using his or her voice.

During the second three months, the baby will begin to babble, seemingly pretending to talk with an ever-increasing vocabulary of sounds. It is here that the first vowels and consonants are practised,and recognisable sounds such as 'mama' might be overheard.

A baby will be able to understand words far sooner than he or she will be able to use them. Towards the end of the first year babies might respond to their name and understand simple instructions such as 'give' and 'no'. They might even have party tricks, where they will follow instructions like 'wave bye-bye' or 'kiss dolly'. Their increasing communication skills mean that it becomes possible for the photographer to give some elementary commands.

▶ LOOK AT ME
As babies start to learn some words, even though they can't say them, they can respond to your instructions. This makes it much easier for the photographer to get the baby to look the right way. Megan can now sit up unaided for long periods, which also improves the photo possibilities.

▶ EXPLORING ON FOOT
Watch for the way that babies and young children will play with their hands or feet, feeling the shape of their fingers, or curling their toes. Here, Megan is thoroughly investigating her toes with her hands, quite unaware of everything else around her. Such scenes make interesting photographic sequences.

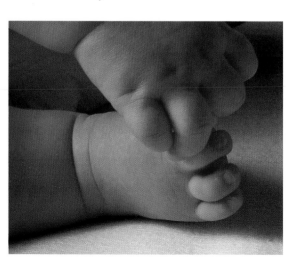

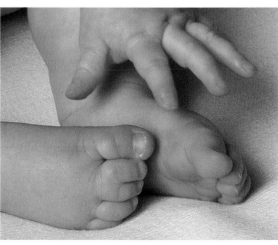

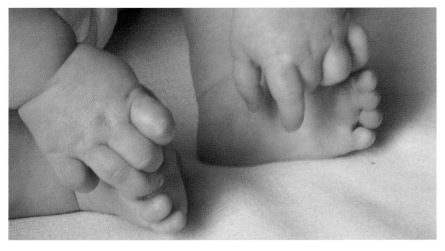

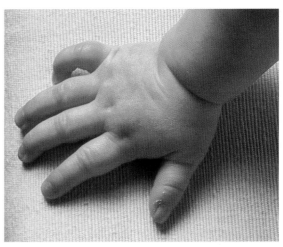

▼**IN PERFECT HANDS**
A baby's hand looks
miniature, even when
there is nothing else in
the composition to
provide a sense of scale.

One year

It might be tempting to think that children acquire certain skills overnight, but often the progression past a new milestone is actually a gradual one, and it might be extremely hard to pinpoint the time when the event occurred in a particular baby's life. Learning to walk is one of these.

The first stage in learning to walk is being able to stand up. By the end of the twelfth month most children will be able to get themselves into an upright position by pulling themselves up against heavy furniture. This is a skill that usually follows fast on the heels of learning to crawl.

As the baby gets more proficient at standing in this way, he or she will be able to use these

◀ **FEAT OF STRENGTH**
Megan is now capable of pulling herself up into the standing position, but her new party trick demands plenty of determination and energy.

▼ **THAT'S ENOUGH**
Megan cannot keep upright for long yet, and her new skill is accompanied by inevitable falls.

▶ **PERFECT PROP**
Two chairs and a plain backdrop create a simple set on which Megan can show off her standing skills. The material used for the background also provides the floor covering, creating a seamless curve that ensures that there are no distracting join lines running along the back of the pictures.

supports as a means of getting around the room. Many babies will be able to use chairs, tables and cupboards in this way near to their first birthday — and although this is not proper walking, they will be well on the road to using their feet to get them from place to place.

Even when they do progress to taking steps on their own, which is most likely to happen around the age of 15 months, it may take much practice before they can manage more than a step or two. The toddler stage of development has begun, but this early "walking" is probably best described as staggering — and there will be plentiful falls along the way.

It will also be a very tiring process — and babies will want to be carried, or wheeled around in their pushchair for some time to come. Their locomotive skills still have a long way to develop — it will be a further 15 months, for instance, before they can run.

◄ TAKEN FOR A RIDE
Many children love to sit on an adult's shoulders, although some find the experience too frightening. Megan enjoys the bird's-eye view, and the pose creates an interesting way in which to photograph her with her father.

▲ MY FIRST CAR
In addition to crawling, and learning to walk, one-year-olds love exercising with baby trikes and cars, making these useful devices to have at hand for a portrait session.

▷ ALL THE FAMILY AGAIN
Full family portraits are a great way of marking birthdays. Comparing it with the shot taken a year before (page 39), this shot shows how much Megan has grown.

To take great pictures it is not enough just to have a camera and a beautiful baby. You also need to understand some of the basics of photography. By being fussy when framing your shots, by looking carefully at the lighting, and by making the most of your camera controls you will soon be taking superb shots all the time.

Basic skills

Composing the shot

The human brain has an amazing ability to be selective about what it sees. The eye may perceive everything in front of you, but you can concentrate solely at looking at just a small part of the scene. A camera cannot be this selective, and the photographer must therefore be careful not to include unnecessary distraction in the picture frame. By getting closer to a subject, by moving round it or zooming it, you can simplify the scene so that it is the subject that has the impact. Sometimes, however, there might be real reasons for including more background or foreground. In photographic composition, it is as important to decide what to leave out of shot as it is to pick what to include.

Once the subject and camera angle are chosen, you then have great scope as to where to place the subject within the frame. Surprisingly, perhaps, having the main focal point in the middle of the shot is rarely the best approach.

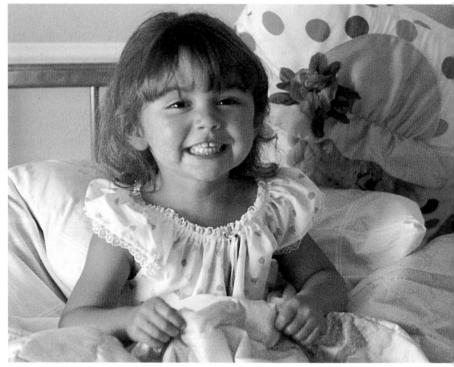

RULE OF THIRDS

▶ **THE EYES HAVE IT**
In this shot it is the child's eyes that are the main focal point of the picture; and these have been placed to coincide at one of the intersections of the grid lines used by the 'rule of thirds'.

In most photographs, you will find that the subject will look best if it is placed slightly away from centre, both horizontally and vertically, if possible.

A more precise, but similar, approach is to use the 'rule of thirds'. Widely used by both photographers and artists, this says that if you were to break the frame up into nine equal rectangles (as left), the best position for the subject, or focal point, would be at one of the four intersections. The key focal point in a portrait is the face or, in the case of a close-up, the person's eyes. Key lines within the frame, such as the horizon, should be placed over one of the four lines making up the grid.

◄ **TOO FAR AWAY**
Don't leave too much room around your subject when framing your shot. Here, the expanse of bed and wall does little to strengthen the picture, and it becomes harder to seen the little girl's face amongst the surrounding detail.

◄ **SYMMETRICAL VIEW**
In some shots you can get away with placing the subject centrally. In this shot, for instance, the girl sits in the middle of the bench. This arrangement stresses the symmetry of the ironwork and the pillars in the distance.

◄ **GETTING IN CLOSER**
By taking that extra step or two towards the subject, the frame is better filled by the child's face, and more of the distracting foreground and background is hidden from view. Instead of moving the camera closer, you could alternatively use a more telephoto zoom setting.

◄ **OFF-CENTRE**
By placing the subject slightly off-centre you create a more unbalanced view, but the eye tends to find this more dynamic and more pleasing. The position of the girl's face roughly corresponds to one of those suggested by the 'rule of thirds'.

◄ **RADICAL FRAMING**
In the shot the position of the girl breaks all the rules, with her face far too close to the edge of the frame. But sometimes it pays to break with convention. The radical composition used here seems to make the girl's decision to stand on the bench look more dramatic and dangerous.

◀ **FRONT CRAWL**
If you want to take pictures of crawling babies, you generally need to crawl too. An alternative approach, though, is to put the child on a raised surface, such as a bed, so that you can get down to his or here eye level without straining your body!

Varying the angle

Varying the height of the camera is one of the many ways in which photographers can add variety to their pictures, but in child photography it has a special significance. It is all too easy to end up photographing children from your own eye level; but this means that you end up looking down on the baby, both literally

▼ **GETTING IN POSITION**
By kneeling or lying to get a lower camera position, you also get a steadier shot, as your elbow can rest on your thigh or on the ground.

and metaphorically. You will get much more pleasing results if you can get the camera down to the child's eye level. In the case of a toddler, this may well mean getting down on your knees, and for a crawling baby it could well mean lying down on the floor.

Whilst you should shoot from the child's head height for most shots, there are times when your pictures can benefit from going even lower. With the camera looking up at the child, he or she will look taller and more grown-up. It is an approach that works well when a child is sitting on a bike, or is dressed up as a favourite action figure.

△ VIEW FROM ABOVE
By shooting downwards from above the child, the picture ends up stressing how short the subject really is. This might be a realistic view, but it does not usually make for intimate portraits.

△ WATCH THE BACKDROP
Lowering the camera height also changes the background of the shot, sometimes for the worse. Here, the bottom of the hedge creates a strong line that breaks the picture in half.

◁ UNIFORM BACKDROP
The angled lens needed for a higher camera position means that the hedge is no longer visible so that the grass creates a plain, uniform background for the portrait.

TURNING THE CAMERA

It is easy to forget, but one of the simplest ways of changing the composition of your pictures is by turning the camera on the side. This then gives you the choice between the 'portrait' or 'landscape' formats which, despite their names, are both equally useful for pictures of babies.

The 'portrait' format is most ideally suited to full-figure shots or shots of people from the waist up; it can be used well with seated and standing subjects. The 'landscape' shot is most used for head-and-shoulder shots, group portraits or for where you deliberately want to show more of the background.

◁ PORTRAIT FORMAT
Turning the camera sideways to create a vertical picture, means that the seated baby fills the frame well.

▽ LANDSCAPE FORMAT
Horizontal framing means that more of the interesting background becomes visible.

Zoom secrets

Zoom lenses are now widely found on both compacts and digital cameras, as well as SLRs. A zoom offers a range of focal lengths; telephoto settings allow you to crop in closer without having to move, whilst wide-angles allow you to fit more into a single frame.

The ideal focal length for the baby photographer is the short telephoto range; on a 35mm-format camera, this means a focal length of between 70 and 140mm. These focal lengths provide distortion-free faces, without having to be too close or too far from the subject. Longer telephoto settings of 200–300mm, however, are useful for candid photographs of toddlers, allowing you to capture their behaviour without them being overly aware of your presence.

Shorter focal lengths, as offered by wide-angle lens settings, can tend to exaggerate facial features if used too close up, but are very handy for showing a baby's surroundings, or for large groups in a confined area.

▶ **MID-TELEPHOTO**
A medium-telephoto lens setting is ideal for taking close-up shots of children's faces without their facial features becoming distorted. For this shot, I used a 135mm lens on a 35mm SLR camera; this focal length is covered on many zooms, including those that are built into some compact and digital cameras.

▶ WIDE-ANGLE EFFECT
A wide-angle lens setting can tend to do strange things to the perspective of portraits when used at close range. However, its beauty is that this makes subjects in the foreground look larger and more dominant than those in the background. At the same time, it shows a wider expanse of background, which can be good if you want to show the setting. In this shot a 35mm wide-angle lens ensures that the baby boy dominates the composition, even though his mother is only just behind him.

KIDS IN CLOSE-UP

It is useful to be familiar with how close a lens can be used to a subject. This minimum focus distance is particularly important when shooting extreme close-ups, such as shots of a newborn baby's hand.

How close you can go will vary immensely depending on the lens and the type of camera you use. Some point-and-shoot film cameras have special macro modes, but although these may allow you to get closer to your subject than usual, they may still give less than satisfactory results.

The macro modes found on many digital cameras are much more impressive, allowing you to focus down to just inches from the subject.

The close-up capabilities of an SLR camera will depend completely on the lens you are using. However, as the lens is interchangeable, you can switch to get better results. A variety of accessories is also available for SLR which will also allow you to increase the magnification so that the image recorded on film is lifesize.

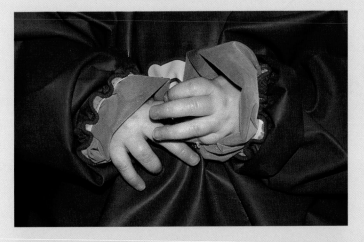

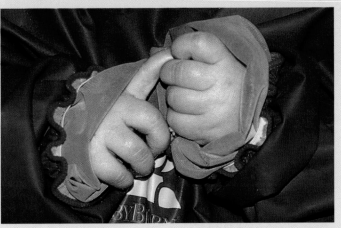

◀ YOU NEED HANDS
If you look closely, you will find that young children are forever playing with their hands and fingers as they learn to use them for finer and finer control. Such scenes make great shots, as long as you can get in close enough.

◀ FINGER EXERCISES
The closer you are to the subject, the less depth of field you have to play with (see pages 73–75), so you need to focus more accurately than usual.

◤FAST SHUTTER SPEED
Bright sunlight shining straight towards us means that an automatic will choose one of the fastest shutter speeds available. The high shutter speed ensures that the running child is caught crisply on film — even the splash of water from the bucket appears frozen in mid-air.

Shutter skill

Shutter speed is one of the two most fundamental creative controls that a photographer has over his or her pictures. Along with aperture, the length of time the shutter stays open does not just affect how light or dark the picture is, it will often change the whole character of a picture.

How much control you have over the shutter speed (or aperture) being used will depend on the type of camera you use. Automatic point-and-shoot models give little creative control. They will adjust the shutter speed for the light level, and may try to ensure it is fast enough so the shot is not affected by the slight movement of the camera during exposure. The only way to manually increase shutter speed may be to switch to a faster, more sensitive film.

With more advanced cameras you can control shutter speed or aperture more directly. Choosing your own shutter speed becomes important when shooting a moving subject such as a toddler running. The faster the image moves across the frame, the faster the shutter speed that is required to freeze the subject. However, you might prefer to deliberately use a slower shutter speed, as the blur may well give a more artistic impression of movement.

TYPES OF CAMERA

The type of camera you choose will depend on your budget, how seriously you want to take your photography, and the size of gadget you want to carry around. There are three basic choices...

◄ COMPACT CAMERA
Point-and-shoots allow hardly any control over shutter speed and aperture. Many have built-in zooms, though, and some offer a limited range of creative effects. Many digital cameras use a compact design.

▼ DIGITAL CAMERA
No film required — pictures are recorded on disk and can be seen directly after being shot. Images are transferred to a PC where they can be printed out, manipulated, emailed and more.

◄ SINGLE LENS REFLEX
SLRs allow wide control over shutter speed and aperture. They also allow you to change lenses, allowing you to pick the zoom or prime lens to suit the subject. Some digital cameras use an SLR design.

▶ SLOW SHUTTER SPEED
The lower the light level, the more the automatic camera is going to choose a slower shutter speed. You can see that this shot has used a slower shutter speed than that used for the similar picture opposite, as the boy's swinging hand appears blurred.

Controlling sharpness

◀ EVERYTHING IN FOCUS
By using a small aperture, practically everything in the picture has been kept sharp, so that you can see the plants in this formal garden as clearly as you can see the little girl.

Aperture is even more important than shutter speed as a creative control, particularly for portraits. Varying the size of hole through which a shot is taken not only varies the amount of light reaching the film, it also affects how much of the picture is sharp.

A lens can only focus at one distance precisely at any one time. But the smaller the aperture you use, the greater the range of distances in front of and behind this point appear to be sharp. The range of distances that appear in focus is known as the depth of field.

A small aperture and maximum depth of field might seem ideal for most pictures, but a large

◀ ▶ SELECTIVE FOCUS
You can control how sharp your background appears by your choice of aperture, your lens setting and your distance from the subject. In this sequence of pictures, a telephoto lens used at close range with a large aperture ensures that only the boy appears sharp.

◀ ▶ DEGREES OF BLUR
Sometimes it is not enough for the background to be out of focus. In the shot on the right, the tree in the background is not sharp, but it is still recognisable and creates a distraction to the subject. This is because a wider zoom setting was used, compared with the shot on the left.

▶**GRADUAL BLUR**
Things become
progressively blurred the
further they are behind
the depth of field zone.
The wide-angle lens
means that the
background in this shot
is recognisable, but the
trees gradually become
less sharp the further
they are behind the boy.

◀**COMPROMISES**
In this shot I wanted to
keep the picturesque
garden in focus.
However, the lighting,
and the need for a fast
enough shutter speed to
avoid camera shake,
meant that I could only
pick an aperture which
left some of the plants
in soft focus.

BLURRING THE BACKGROUND

With most pictures of babies you want to use depth of field to make the background disappear so that it doesn't distract from the subject. Here are some of the main ways that you achieve this aim, whatever camera you own:

Use a wider aperture. If you have an auto-only camera you have no choice here, but you can force the camera to use a wider aperture by choosing a slower film, or by decreasing the brightness (moving to a less sunny part of the garden, say).

Get closer to the subject — this will also crop out more of the background.

Use a longer zoom setting. This is the best way of restricting depth of field on a compact or digital camera with a built-in zoom. Use the longest zoom setting available. If buying a point-and-shoot camera, buy one with the longest zoom you can afford, as this gives more indirect control of depth of field.

One of the simplest ways of blurring the background is to increase the distance between the subject and the background. You can't move the walls, of course, but you can move the baby further into the room.

aperture can be used to ensure that the subject really stands out from its surroundings by throwing foreground and background out of focus. There is also the trade-off between shutter speed and the light level, which will often mean that you don't have a completely free choice as to the aperture you use.

Aperture, however, is only one of three main factors that affect depth of field. The others are the focal length of the lens you use, and the distance that you focus at.

The wider the lens you use, the more depth of field you are likely to have. This is one of the

▶ TELEPHOTO BLUR
If you focus on a child's face, anything else in the picture that is the same distance away is also going to be sharp. Here, the wall and window frame in the foreground would have been sharp, whatever lens or aperture I had used. Note that the far wall of the ruined cottage, however, is out of focus.

▼ SEEING DEEPER
Although this is a similar shot to that on the left, I have moved further back and zoomed out so as to include the sax-playing mum in the picture. This has meant that depth of field has been increased, even though it was not necessary for the shot. This means the far wall, behind the boy's head, now appears much sharper than before.

reasons why short telephoto lenses are favoured for portraits of children, as they allow you to blur the background more easily.

The other factor for controlling depth of field is where you focus the lens. The greater the distance the lens is focused at, the greater the depth of field. When you are close to the subject, it essential that you focus the camera more accurately. Focusing on the subject roughly is not enough, as it might not be possible to keep the whole figure or face in focus. The one part of the face that needs to be sharp is the eyes, and this is where you should focus.

Finding simple backdrops

Although you can simplify any background using depth of field, the amount of control you have in this area is often limited. It is best, therefore, to pick a plain background in the first place so that, whatever lens setting or aperture you use, it will not distract from the subject. Ideally this background will have little or no pattern; it will also be neutral in colour, or will tone with the

◀ **PLAIN BEDSPREAD**
A white bedspread makes a simple but effective backdrop against which to shoot a small child. Drape the material so that it rises behind the subject and creates a seamless, unbroken background to the shot.

▶ **IN THE SHADES**
Don't forget that with young children it is you who decide where they stand or sit, so you have a much freer choice of background than you would with some photographic subjects. To photograph this toddler with her shades, I persuaded her to stand in front of this plain blue tent.

clothes that the child is wearing.

The professional can set up rolls of coloured paper, or specially-painted screens, that can be used as a plain background against which to pose the subjects. The expense may stop the amateur going to such extremes, but it is still worth spending your time finding and erecting, a plain canvas. A large white sheet, for instance, hung from a wall and then draped over the floor will create an ideal 'cove' in which to shoot a crawling baby; you can use a large tarpaulin in a similar way. Look also for walls or curtains that can be used as impromptu backdrops.

◢ CLUTTER ALL AROUND
Compare this shot with the one on the left. The one below may be a more representative view of the clutter and equipment that are needed when going on holiday with a toddler, but most people will probably prefer the simpler composition for their own baby album.

◢ BELOW YOUR FEET
If you can't find an uncluttered background around you, look down. Floorboards, carpet, paving, grass — all offer large continuous backdrops to shoot against. The only disadvantage is that you are forced to shoot downwards.

Complex backdrops

Simple backgrounds may be best, but they are not always possible — or wanted. Often kids do things that you have to catch on film quickly and there's no time to move them. In any case, you often need to shoot candidly, as alerting the child to your presence will bring that magic moment to an end.

The background may also be necessary for the story you are trying to tell. On a visit to the zoo, it is only natural to want to picture the child with animals in the background. A famous landmark similarly sets the scene for a holiday photograph. You may simply want to show your home in more detail, so that when they grow up the children will see the places where they lived.

⊿ ON THE NET
A playground in the background might suit this shot of the girl climbing a cargo net. But the foreground is already packed with information, so I decided to throw the backdrop well out of focus.

▶ LEADING THE EYE
Picnic tables make a busy backdrop, and it was impossible to frame the shot so as to hide them. Instead, I composed the shot so that the line of the table in the foreground leads the eye into the picture and towards the child's face.

Backgrounds can also be used to create a mood. A flower garden can suggest peace and tranquillity, as long as it is matched by a tranquil pose. A fairground can be used to suggest excitement and could be used as a backdrop to a shot of a child having fun holding a helium balloon or wearing a mask. Backgrounds can sometimes be even more complementary to subject matter — a stately home would make a great backdrop for a shot of a little girl dressed as a princess.

△ TROMPE L'OEIL
Murals and large paintings are very effective backdrops for photographs, creating a theatrical set in which to pose your subjects.

SOFTENING THE EFFECT

Elaborate fabrics might suit your interior decor, but they can be quite overpowering when used as backdrops to your photographs. But you can get away with heavily patterned materials if they are thrown slightly out of focus. The easiest way of doing this is to increase the distance between the child and the background.

△ POWERFUL PRESENCE
With the flowery backdrop placed immediately behind the subject, it tends to clash with the girl's patterned dress.

◁ FORWARD THINKING
By bringing the baby just a couple of feet forward, the backdrop now appears must softer in the picture, and now complements the dress rather than clashing with it.

Framed within the frame

Although you can get closer to a subject and can change camera position, the way a picture is framed is to some extent dictated by the camera that you use. The sides of the frame cannot usually be altered so that the subject fits in better, so you are stuck with a rectangle with fixed proportions.

One way of changing this, however, is to look for natural frames in which to enclose your picture — foreground elements that make a differently shaped aperture through which to see the child. Windows and doorways, for instance, make great secondary frames in which to pose portraits. They add an interesting design to the shot, alter the effective dimensions of the photograph, and can often be used to hide other distracting elements in the scene.

◤ **CLIMBING FRAME**
A circular opening on a piece of playground equipment creates an unusual and eye-catching frame for a picture of a child. Adventure parks offer a great range of such natural frames.

◀ **FOCUS OF ATTENTION**
Take care when taking pictures through glass, as the autofocus system of the camera could well focus on the surface of the glass rather than on the subject behind.

▲ WINDOW BOX
A sash window with an attractive container planted with herbs makes an attractive setting for a shot of mother and child.

▶ PUT TO FULL USE
Once you have found a good setting, use it for other portraits and groupings. This time it is grandmother's turn to hold the baby.

▶ CLINGING ON
Natural frames not only break up the picture in different ways, they often create an impression of depth that can be missing from a two-dimensional print. Here, a car window creates a semi-transparent barrier that splits the picture into two distinct halves.

Bright colours

Colour is one of the most powerful elements in photographic composition. Some colours attract the eye far more strongly than others; put just a splash of red in a shot, and you are drawn to this area first.

The combination of hues also makes a difference — vibrant combinations create impact, whilst pastel shades that tone together well create a more tranquil composition.

It might seem that you have little control over the colours in your baby pictures, but you have far more influence than in most forms of photography. You can choose or suggest the clothes that the young child wears, picking items that stand out boldly, perhaps, or going for colours that complement the background. You can also select the background to suit the colour of your subject's clothes and add finishing touches with the props and accessories.

◢ FINISHING TOUCHES
A change of clothes may not always be available, so you may have to make the best of what they have on. However, you can always add colourful accents with props such as hats, umbrellas and balloons.

◣ VISUAL UNITY
With group shots it pays for each person to wear similar colours, as this will create a visual bond between the individuals, which can help to stress the family link. Here mum, dad and baby have all worn clothes from the red/purple end of the spectrum.

▶ **BIG MAC**
A bright statue of Ronald McDonald made an irresistible centrepiece for a child portrait. Marketing men know that young children love bright colours, so merchandise, toys or advertising aimed for little eyes almost always make extensive use of the richest primaries.

◀ **EYE-CATCHING ATTIRE**
Red and yellow are two colours that leap out of photographs, grabbing the attention of the viewer. By careful choice of clothes, you can use colour in this way to create visual impact in practically any child portrait. The great advantage of shooting your own children is that you have direct control over their wardrobe.

▲ HIGH-KEY PORTRAIT
One of the attractions of black-and-white film is that it is easy to develop and print yourself. This then gives you an incredible amount of creative control over the results. When printing, for example, you can change the contrast, or lighten and darken selective parts of the image. In this shot, I have opted for a high-key approach in the darkroom , with the choice of contrast and exposure allowing the light tones to dominate.

Black and white

Colour film might be the most popular choice for family pictures, but there is a lot to be said for occasionally shooting pictures in black and white. Portraits are particularly successful in monochrome, as it immediately eliminates the distraction of colour created by clashing clothing or a busy background. With tone alone, the picture concentrates on the shape of the face, the expression and the texture of the skin.

Black and white can also be an excellent remedy when a child has a rash or spots, as these become far less obvious when shown in black and white. The film can also come to the rescue when trying to use normal room lighting indoors. With colour film, bulb or strip lighting creates pictures that are tinged orange or green. With black and white this is not a problem, allowing you to use whatever lighting you have available to boost the illumination level.

DIGITAL DARKROOM

Digital cameras do not give you the choice of different films for different purposes, as images are recorded electronically using a fixed CCD chip that converts the light into an electrical signal.

Many digital cameras, however, offer a special mode, allowing you to record the image in black and white, rather than in colour. The camera may even allow you to record images in sepia, thus recreating the old-fashioned tinted picture style of yesteryear (as used for the introductory shot shown on page 6).

However, it is very easy to turn colour digital images into black-and-white ones after they are taken. This is done in a fraction of a second with most image manipulation software, and toned effects can be added just as easily.

Most digital photographers, therefore, shoot portraits in colour and then convert them to black and white when required on the computer. This then always gives them a choice between the two different approaches.

◤ **SIMPLIFY THE SCENE**
A black-and-white shot allows the composition to concentrate on form, pattern, shape and texture. Distracting colours — such as the yellow walls, brown floor and orange bedspread in this scene — are completely hidden from view.

◀ **CHANGING TONES**
Black and white can be harder to work with than colour film, simply because it is not easy to visualise what the result will look like. The colour of objects must still be taken into consideration, as the darkness of tone can appear different on film than it does to the human eye. Red and blue appear lighter, whilst the green of the grasss in this shot has become darker.

Getting the right expression

Even if the exposure is perfect and the camera angle spot-on, it is still easy to end up with disappointing pictures. People move, and the expression they make during the split second that the shutter is open might be less than photogenic. They may blink at the wrong moment, frown or move their head. Dealing with babies is more difficult, as they are less able to respond to your instructions.

There are no easy routes to the perfect pose, but you can increase your chances of success. Keep each session short, so the child doesn't get bored, ensuring everything is ready in advance. Keep talking, singing or joking with the child so that they feel relaxed. Young babies will need to see a familiar face, and you may need to shoot over a parent's shoulder so that the happy face seems to be looking at the camera.

▶ **PERFECT POSE**
Not every shot you will take will be great, because a child's face is constantly changing in expression. With digital cameras you can check after each shot whether the pose was good; with film you need to take as many shots as possible to ensure a successful picture like this one.

▶ **HANDS OFF**
Hands can look particularly awkward in pictures, and it is often a good idea to get a child to link his or her hands together in front so that they make a neat arrangement. Alternatively, they can be linked behind the child, so that they do not interfere with the composition at all — this is a particularly useful trick with group shots.

▶ **HANDS ON**
The little boy's hands obscure the shot in these two pictures. If this is a particularly typical pose of the child, then the pictures will appeal to relatives more, than if this is just nervous behaviour in front of camera.

FRAMING TIPS

Be careful how you frame up the human figure — if the bottom of the shot cuts through the neck or knees of a person, the results can look very unnatural.

For close-ups of faces, ensure the top of the head is in shot, and that you include the top of the shoulders.

For fuller shots, cut off the shot at the waist or thigh, rather than at the elbows or knees.

▶ SMILE PLEASE!

Children can smile in so many different ways, but not all of these will be characteristic of the child. Unless you know the child well, it will be almost impossible to tell which is which.

▶ FUNNY FACES

Make your portrait sessions fun by letting the child pull faces for the camera. Some of these will make amusing studies, and the antics will also help to persuade the child that having your picture taken doesn't have to be serious and boring.

Flying babies

Until they learn to run and jump, children offer little scope for action photography. But dramatic shots are not impossible. From an early age, adults will pick up babies and gently toss them into the air. As if preparing themselves for the thrills of the adventure park, tots normally love the sensation of been lifted up high, 'dropped' suddenly, and spun around. Often the game becomes more and more boisterous, until the day comes that the child is too heavy for the adult to lift in this way.

Such scenes make great pictures, not just because of the way in which they add drama and movement to portraits. They are also work well because of the way the pose emphasises the strong bond between a child and the adult, whether it be a father, uncle or family friend. The two will look as they are both enjoying themselves together, and the pose will highlight the trust the child has in the adult.

The shot can also be useful simply because it allows you to frame up the shot using the sky as a backdrop. This then provides a plain, natural background for the shot, which can otherwise be difficult to find (see pages 76–79). You should be aware, though, that the sky can be significantly brighter than the child in the foreground, and this may lead to exposure difficulties. The camera angle you choose, therefore, can be all-important.

▲ CLEAR SKIES
Forget about using rolls of paper in the studio — a clear sky makes a perfectly graduated backdrop against which to frame a child. However, you need to get the camera significantly lower than the child to frame them against this blue background, so the child needs to be raised up high.

▷ UP WE GO
Not only do 'flying baby' shots help convey the strong bond between child and adult, the game also keeps both subjects occupied. This means you can shoot a sequence of pictures without them being overly aware of the camera.

▶ SILHOUETTE

A blue sky can be significantly brighter than the foreground, particularly if the subject is in shadow, or if you are facing towards the sun. If you then expose for the sky, you will end up with a silhouette. Although you can't see faces clearly, the strong shapes can still make great photographs.

▶ SPOTLIGHT

It can be amazing just what a difference a small change in subject position or camera angle can make to a picture. By moving just slightly, the man and baby are now in sunlight, allowing us to see their faces that much more clearly.

◀ FAST REACTIONS

For a shot like this, you need a shutter speed of at least 1/250sec to ensure that the child is caught reasonably crisply on film. You also need to be sure that the picture is sharp, and it may pay to pre-focus the camera at a suitable distance, so that the lens is already ready when the baby comes into view. This allows you to concentrate on pressing the shutter button at the right time.

Family groups

The secret with trying to shoot family groups is not to try to over-regulate the proceedings. The formal style of portrait used from the Victorian era onwards can be quite impossible to achieve with today's independently minded children. Although it is nice to see everyone dressed up all spick and span, a freestyle approach is often easier.

You don't need to have everyone in a perfectly straight line, but it does make sense to have the smaller members of the family near the front. Toddlers and babies are usually best held by the adults, so that they stay in position.

It is customary for everyone to be looking at the camera in these situations, but this is not essential. If they are looking at each other, this works just as well. To keep young minds from wandering, I find it useful to get them to tell a story — or, even better, to persuade everyone to sing a favourite nursery song.

▶ **EYE TO EYE**
Babies are frequently at their best behaviour when they can actually see the face of the person holding them. Taking photographs, therefore, where the mother and child are directly facing each other is likely to help provide a stress-free picture-taking session.

SAFETY IN NUMBERS

The more people you have in a photograph together, the greater the chance that one of them is frowning or has their eyes closed. Stage-managing a formal portrait means the photographer needs to be authoritative, yet good-tempered. But to ensure that everyone is happy with the results, you need to take as many different exposures as you can before everyone gets restless.

▶UNHAPPY FACES
It is impossible to ensure that everyone is smiling, facing the right way, and has their eyes open in every picture. You need to accept that some shots won't work, and shoot plenty of film.

◀VARY THE POSE
Get the subjects to change positions, and do different things during the shoot, so that they are kept involved. Here the parents were asked to look at their children, to create a less formal, but charming, study.

▲ MUTUAL DISTRACTION
Another ploy for keeping subjects from looking bored whilst they are being photographed together, is to get them involved in an activity together, such as reading a book, playing with a puzzle or making cakes.

▼ BONNY BABY CONTEST
A new baby means that the mother will make new friends at post-natal classes, toddler groups and so on. These get-togethers provide great shots of the baby's own first friends. This shot was taken at a baby beauty pageant.

▶THE WINNING SHOT
With film cameras, it is impossible to see exactly what expressions you have caught on camera until the film has been processed. The photographer needs to do his or her best on every single frame.

◄ **GOING TO WASTE**
This wastebin made a
perfect photogenic
playpen for this set-up
shot. The bright blue
colour contrasts nicely
with the elegant red hat.
Planters and large
flowerpots could be
used in a similar way.

▲ **UP ON THE ROOF**
The device you use to
keep a child in one place
will have more relevance
if it is something he or
she is used to playing
with. Here, the girl
proudly poses on top of
her dolls' house.

On the spot

Once a baby has learnt to crawl, shots of him or her alone become more difficult to stage-manage. When shot with a parent babies can be held in position, but on their own they will wander off away from the perfect lighting and background, or come to check out the camera. You need something that confines them to a particular spot, so they can't escape so readily as you wait for the perfect expression. A playpen will not do as it will not look good on film. The perfect solution is something like a rocking horse – fun for the child to sit on, but doesn't move. You don't need anything as grandiose, though. Toddlers love to sit in boxes and bowls, which can be chosen so they look good on camera. These can be positioned where you want them, and then put in place when you are ready.

PLAIN BACKDROPS

When children are older, you can get them to pose practically anywhere. All you need to do is to ask them to get into position. Toddlers are curious about everything around them, and will not stand still for more than a few seconds. Traditionally, photographers use rolls of paper (bought from professional photographic stores) to create a plain floor and background for portraits. This can be mimicked using a large white sheet, or by using rolls of wallpaper (used back to front so the pattern does not show). This can work well for shots of babies. However, once the child is old enough to crawl, they have precious little incentive to stay on this empty area for very long, so you need to act quick if you want to try this approach.

▶ **IN POSITION**
A roll of plain paper makes a simple and effective backdrop for portraits...

◀ **WANDERING OFF**
...but toddlers do not stay still for long, and they will soon stray from the spot!

◀ **IN THE TUB**
Washing-up bowls and large cooking pots make useful impromptu baths. The set-up has the advantage that the warm water will be comforting to a young child or baby, as well as giving them something to play with.

▼ SEEING THE SIGHTS
A child's buggy is like a sight-seeing bus — from here all the attractions are seen. By using wide-angle framing, you can not only see the child, but also the location that is being visited.

Have chair, will travel

For the first two or three years, a baby will spend much of his or her time being confined to a chair. Whether in the form of a pram, pushchair, buggy or car seat, one of these devices will accompany the child whenever he or she leaves the house. These wheeled chariots will help transport them on all their early outings, holidays and promenades.

Such pieces of machinery may not seem particularly photogenic. However, these travelling seats are an integral part of the child's

early years , and you should not be afraid to include them in your pictures. Some, in fact, look more stylish in pictures than others, but whatever they look like, they also serve a useful photographic purpose. They can be positioned (like the bowls and pots on pages 92–93) against the background, and in the lighting, of your choice. Furthermore, because the child is strapped in he or she can not come to harm or escape the attention of your camera.

▲ DIAGONAL LINES
Diagonal lines form a useful compositional trick. They break up the squared-off shape forced on us by the viewfinder, and they lead the eye across the picture. Here, the triangular shape of the wall seems to echo the shape of the three-wheeled buggy.

◄ ME AND MY SHADOW
The shape of subjects always becomes more apparent when shown in silhouette. Here, the outlines of the mother, child and buggy are emphasised in this way and then repeated in their shadows on the watery sand.

▶ RESTING PLACE
When children really need the rest, they can fall asleep practically anywhere. A pushchair is not just a carriage, it often turns into a portable cot. Here, two siblings get some welcome shut-eye.

▼ NEW AND OLD
Here, the ultra-modern design of a three-wheeled buggy is juxtaposed against the half-timbered architecture of a Tudor building. Such pictures provide mementoes of the places that a baby visited in his or her first years.

◀ HEIRLOOM
Prams, like clothes and cars, change in design and fashion over the years. This old model has probably been passed down through the family, but is still providing good service.

Sun and shadow

I t is not just how much light there is that is important when taking pictures — the quality of the light also counts. One of the most important factors that dictates quality is how hard or soft the light is. In direct sunlight, a subject creates hard, distinct shadows.

Sunlight is not always direct, though; it bounces off buildings and the ground, scattering as it gets reflected. It passes through clouds, which diffract the light in a thousand different directions. This is known as soft, or indirect, light and creates less distinct shadows. There are pros and cons to both types of lighting. With soft lighting you can see faces clearly, without heavy shadows under people's eyes and noses. However, it can also be lifeless, giving drab results. Direct lighting gives much brighter pictures which show detail and colour much better. Choosing which you use makes a great difference to the impact of your pictures.

◀ DIRECT SUNLIGHT
With no cloud overhead, the sun streams down, lighting up some parts of the child's face and body, whilst throwing others into dark shadow.

▶ INDIRECT LIGHTING
With softer sunlight, the shadows are far less distinct than before, so that we can see the face far more clearly. However, the picture does not have as much punch as before. Notice how the colour of the boy's shorts now appears to be a less bright tone than before.

▶ SUNNY SPELLS

The quality of light can vary outdoors from one second to the next. In this shot, the rays break through a gap in the clouds, providing direct lighting. Note the face is in half-shadow — some light still reaches the features, but not distinctly.

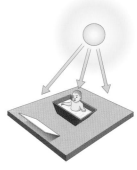

▶ OVERCAST

A few minutes later, and the clouds overhead are now heavier, scattering the light more broadly. The overall effect is that the bright highlights and dark shadows have practically disappeared from the picture, revealing the face clearly.

MATTERS OF DEGREE

Fortunately, you rarely have to use soft or hard light alone for portraits. The sunlight may be direct, but the shadow areas are usually partially lit by softer, reflected light. This gives the best of both worlds — the shadows are not too heavy on the face, whilst the portrait is lifted by the warmth and colour of the direct sunlight.

◀ SEMI-DIFFUSE LIGHT

You can tell from the bright area on the baby's left cheek that the lighting is coming from this direction. But the other cheek is not in shadow, it is only slightly darker than the other side of the face. This is because it is being lit by light reflected back from a wall.

Looking into the light

he other main factor that affects the quality of light is its direction. By varying the angle of the sun in relation to the subject, you change both the position of the shadows and the character of the picture.

Standing with the sun behind you, you are using what is known as frontal lighting. This is frequently the best natural lighting to use for many types of photography as shadows are thrown behind the subject, where you can't see them. This is usually the best angle of light to maximise the colour in a scene.

The main disadvantage of this lighting can be that the absence of shadows means that there is little information to imply the three-dimensional shape of the subject through its form and texture. However, if the light is not quite straight on, this is less of a problem. Also, as human faces are not flat surfaces, this is less of an obstacle than with some forms of photography.

◣ BRIGHT HIGHLIGHTS
Using light from a bright window over my left shoulder, the baby's face is fairly evenly illuminated by the direct sunlight. Note, however, that as different parts of the face and clothes are at different angles to the light, there is still some shadow on the mother's face.

◪ SOFT TOUCH
Frontal lighting is not always harsh and direct. In this shot, the sun was behind the camera, even though it was obscured by light cloud. This gives even lighting, minimal shadow and reasonable colour saturation.

BRIGHT EYES
Frontal lighting can prove a problem with portraits if the sunlight is too bright or too direct, because people screw their eyes up. It is usually better, therefore, to wait for some partial cloud cover, so that the eyes look more relaxed.

A LATE START
Frontal lighting usually works best outdoors late in the afternoon or first thing in the morning. At these times of the day, the sunlight is less intense and is diffused more by the atmosphere, and because the sun is lower you avoid ugly shadows under the nose and eyes.

▶ WINDOW DRAPES
Here, sidelight is provided by a window to the side of the toddler. If the sunlight is too bright in these situations, it is possible to diffuse the light sufficiently by closing the blinds slightly, partially drawing the curtains, or by draping netting over the windows.

Adding the third dimension

◀ TRUE TO FORM
In this shot, the plant pot in the background neatly illustrates the effect of sidelighting. It is the gradation of tones, from the bright area on the right side of the pot to the darker shadows on the left-hand side, that tells us about the three-dimensional shape of the container. The same lighting conditions give good form to the boy's face.

The weakness of photographs is that they are two-dimensional — there is no direct information about depth. This missing dimension is only implied by clues left in the picture, and, in particular, on how the shadows fall. Imagine a perfect sphere: with no shadows, it would appear as a flat circle in the shot. Also you would have little idea whether its surface was smooth or pitted like an orange. In short, there would be no clues to form or texture.

The best way of showing these qualities in a portrait is with sidelighting. As the light sweeps across the subject, some parts of the head and

▼DRAMATIC EFFECT
With direct sidelighting, there is a strong contrast between light and shade. Much of the face is obscured, and results are not flattering. The moody results are popular for portraits of adults, and occasionally can prove successful with children.

◢ TURNED TO THE LIGHT
Although the teddy and dressing gown are obviously sidelit, the girl's face is more evenly illuminated with frontal lighting, as she is facing the window.

▷ PERFECT SKIN
Soft sidelighting shows off the smooth, soft and unblemished skin of young children.

body are are brightly lit whilst others are in deep shadow. It is these, and the areas in between, that tell us about the smoothness of a baby's face and the curves of his or her chubby cheeks.

Sidelighting does not work well if the light is too direct. It needs to be sufficiently softened so that the shadow areas are not so black that key parts of the face are lost from view.

Flash effects

Built-in flashguns mean that it is possible to take pictures of children whatever the weather and time of day. But it is important that you are aware of the limitations. To begin with, the position and design of the flash means that the lighting provided is very direct, and very frontal, which is less than ideal for portraits. There is also the danger that if the subject is near to the background, the flash will create a harsh black outline around the subject.

Flash is also not very effective over long distances. This is not such a problem, as you can get close to the child. But it means that backgrounds often appear unnaturally dark.

Those using SLR cameras with separate flashguns can exercise greater control over the character of the lighting, either by using the flash away from the camera to create slight sidelighting effects or by bouncing the light off nearby walls or diffusing it to illuminate the subject in a softer manner.

▶ **BOUNCE FLASH**
Optional flashguns for SLR cameras allow you to tilt and swivel the flashhead, so that you can bounce the light off a neutral-coloured surface such as a wall or ceiling. This means the flash is softened, creating less distinct shadows. It also avoids reflections from shiny surfaces, such as those of the sunglasses worn by this little boy.

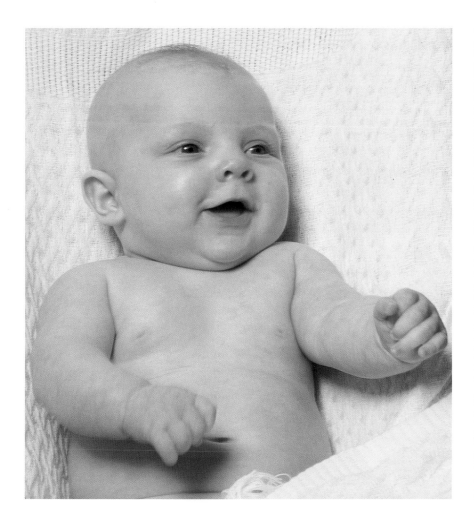

CURSE OF THE RED-EYE

A major drawback with using flash for portraits is the risk of red-eye. This is caused by the flash reflecting off the retina, showing up blood vessels in the eye; the pupils of the eye then look red, rather than black. There are some solutions::

Many compact cameras, and some SLRs with built-in flash units, have a special flash setting to reduce the effect. This uses a pre-flash which forces the child's pupils to contract before the shot is actually taken. However, the delay between pressing the shutter and the exposure means spontaneous shots are impossible.

The simplest solution is to get closer to the child; the longer the lens you use, the more you will have problems with red-eye.

If you have an SLR with a separate flashgun, buy a bracket or lead that lets you to increase the distance between the lens and flash tube.

Turn on more lights in the room.

Digital manipulation software will let you paint the pupils a more natural colour. You can achieve a similar result with a black thin-tipped waterproof marker pen; carefully dab the red parts of the print a point at a time.

◣ SHADOW OUTLINE
On-camera flash creates hard shadows, and although these fall behind the subject, these can create dark outlines around the subject if the child is particularly close to the background. In this shot, you can see a heavy shadow to the right of the baby's head, and under his arms.

▶ DIMINISHING RETURNS
If some areas of the frame are further away from the camera than others, they will appear darker: you can't light them evenly with a single flash. In this shot, the girl appears well exposed, but the background appears unnaturally dark.

Fill-in flash

Flash is not just useful after dark or when indoors; it can also prove surprisingly useful in daylight. When used in this way, it is known as fill-in flash. The existing sunlight still has a predominant effect on the scene, but the flash can change the contrast of the lighting, providing a balance or punch to your shots that would otherwise not be possible. Even on compact cameras, there is usually a facility to turn the flash on manually.

There are two main uses for fill-in flash. On sunny days, with strong direct sidelight or backlight, a burst of flash will soften or eliminate harsh shadows across the face. The flash effectively reduces the contrast of the shot, making for a more evenly lit exposure.

Fill-in flash has the opposite effect on dull, overcast days. Here, the heavily diffused sunlight tends to create pictures with dull, muted colours. A burst of flash here increases contrast, beefs up the colour back in the scene and adds a sparkle of light to a child's eyes.

◢ DISSOLVING SHADOWS
On a bright, sunny day, a burst of flash fills in most of the heavy shadows that you would normally expect with this sidelit portrait. The boy is effectively being lit from two different directions. The flash unit, however, only has a range of under 2m (6ft), so you need to be close to the child.

◀ **NO FLASH**
Overcast conditions mean that portraits can appear to be rather grey, with people failing to stand out well from the background.

▶ **WITH FILL-IN FLASH**
With a burst of flash, the subject is much more brightly lit. Note how the shadows in the eye sockets have been eliminated, and how there are now bright catchlights in both the mother's and baby's eyes.

WHITE SHEETS AND MIRRORS

Whilst fill-in flash can prove a useful tool for changing the lighting characteristics of a daylit scene, there is another extremely important way of filling in the shadows and changing the quality of the lighting. Reflectors allow you simply to bounce back light into the darker side of the face, softening the overall effect of the lighting.

Shop-bought reflectors are usually collapsible, circular affairs that can easily be carried around, folding into a pouch when not in use. But there is no need to go to this expense. A large sheet of white card, for instance, will often serve just as well.

With sidelit portraits of children, it is easy to erect a white sheet on the unlit side of the child, which can be draped over a clothes horse or over the backs of a couple of chairs. This will then bounce back light from the window into the shadow areas. You don't lose the shadows entirely, but you reduce the harshness of the direct light.

A white sheet also makes a very efficient and low-cost diffuser. In strong sunlight, this can be held out as a light screen by two assistants and will soften the light significantly.

An even more efficient reflector is a mirror, which will bounce back even more light to fill in the shadows. With all reflectors, the bigger the better; it should be bigger than the child. Slight changes to the angle of the mirror will change the effect.

Outdoors, you can light up a face surprisingly effectively by getting a helper to hold a newspaper or open book under the chin of the child. You then crop in tightly on the face. This approach brightens up the features in poor light and softens harsh shadows in hard, direct light.

◀ **NO REFLECTOR**
Although lit from windows on three sides, the face of the little girl is bathed in shadow.

◀ **MIRROR MAGIC**
By placing a large mirror to the right-hand side of the camera and just out of view, the portrait is transformed. The mirror was carefully angled so that it created a shaft of reflected light that spotlit the face of the girl perfectly.

The newborn babe

▶ **KEEP THINGS SIMPLE**
The easiest way to simplify the composition in a busy maternity ward is to take advantage of the white sheets on the bed as a background, and then stand on a chair to get an elevated camera angle. Here, the mother also wears white so that the baby can be seen that much more clearly.

▼ **HAND IN HAND**
Including mother or father in the shot can help to give a sense of scale to the picture. Only by comparing the newborn baby's hands with those of his mother can we get an idea of just how small his hands are.

Babies rarely look at their best when they are first born. Their bodies are often recovering from the rigours of birth, and their skin can either appear very red for the first few days, or can appear yellow with jaundice. However, to the family the child is still a beautiful miracle. It is only natural, therefore, to want to catch the first moments on film, if only so that all those friends, neighbours and colleagues can be shown pictures of the new arrival as soon as possible.

There are obvious difficulties in shooting newborn babies. A hospital is a busy place — there is restricted space, and the demands of doctors and nurses must come first. There is also a lot of clutter and medical equipment around that will look out of place in the family album.

Many people also worry about using flash with newborn babies. Sudden bursts of light may well disturb a resting child, so you might feel more comfortable using a high-speed film (ISO1600 or ISO3200) so that flash is unnecessary.

YOU'VE GOT MAIL

There are always dozens of people to tell when a new baby is born in the family. One of the quickest ways of passing around family news is via email. Rather than just sending an announcement with birthday, weight and names, you could also transmit a picture. Scan the picture into your computer (if it is not a digital image), saving it in JPEG (.jpg) format. This will ensure that the vast majority of users will be able to open the image with little problem. Do not send large file sizes — use image software to compress the image down to 100–200KB so the shot doesn't take too long to download.

◀ **IN THE PICTURE**
**Email is a cost-free way
of giving baby pictures
to friends and family.**

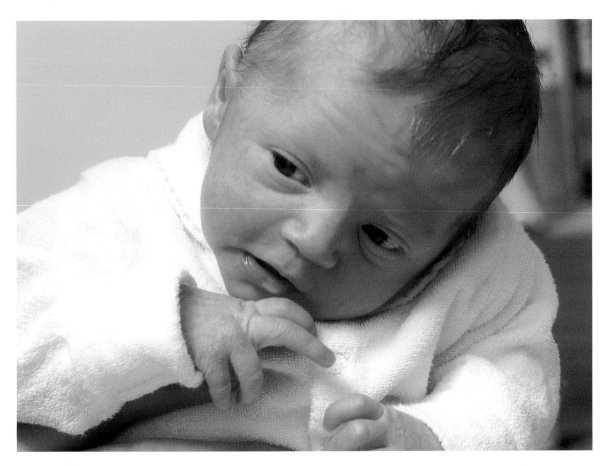

◀ **ACT QUICKLY**
**Don't forget that both
baby and mother will be
very tired after their
ordeal. Get every-
thing ready in advance,
so that you do not need
to keep them posing
for more than a few
minutes.**

Bathtime

Children discover soon enough that washing is a chore that is best avoided. But before they learn to turn away from a wet flannel. babies and toddlers can find bathtime one of the most enjoyable of their daily rituals. Bathtime can be a time of immense freedom and pleasure for them. They can splash, play with plastic ducks and boats, and play with soap suds. As long as parents are relaxed about water going all over the place, the relaxation and excitement of the child will lead to some fantastic pictures.

Parents should be aware, however, that in today's climate of opinion, pictures of children innocently playing with no clothes on are no longer viewed as acceptable in some countries. Whilst nudity was once perfectly normal in a baby album, it is now frowned upon — and can lead to difficulties at processing laboratories. At bathtime, therefore, it pays to use the camera with care. My suggestion is to to be generous with the bubble bath — the foam will keep both baby and the moral majority happy.

◄ **ACTION SEQUENCE**
The confines of the bathroom, and the reliance on flash, may mean that individual shots are not particularly strong. Instead, by putting together a sequence of such events, you capture the excitement of the activity, without putting too much emphasis on an individual frame. The pictures could be mounted in an album in such sequences.

OUT IN THE OPEN

Most of us think of bathtime as being an indoor event, but in the right weather there is no reason why babies can not be bathed outdoors.

The advantage of this is that you get much better natural lighting, because bathrooms rarely have much window light.

It also means that the child can splash to his or her heart's content without any worry about wet carpets and ruined furnishings.

A baby bath, a big bowl or even a large saucepan can be used for babies, particularly when they are old enough to sit up on their own.

Fill the container with warm, soapy water so that it won't be a shock for the child to get into.

You can take similar pictures of older children by using a paddling pool.

◄ TOP-UP TIME
Have plenty more warm, soapy water on hand, so that the child does not get cold.

► SOAP OPERA
Bubble bath will provide children with fun for years, and also acts as a simple way of making your pictures decent enough to avoid any embarrassment, now or in the future.

First steps

Learning to walk is one of the key milestones in a baby's development. But, contrary to popular opinion, it rarely happens overnight. Even when children suddenly take their first step, it will take lots of practice before they are anywhere near steady on their legs. They will stagger, they will fall and they will revert to crawling around whenever they get tired. The process may begin at the age of around nine months with some adventurous babies, but may well be left until the age of 18 months by others.

As it is a gradual transformation from crawling on all fours to walking on two legs, the photographer in the family should feel under no pressure to catch the very first steps made. There will be plenty of other early attempts, which will look just as convincing in your pictures. To catch these scenes of bold determination it is usually best to use a telephoto lens setting, so you can track their progress without getting in their way.

◤ **DUSTY ROAD**
A stony path is more like an obstacle course to anyone without shoes, but this young walker combines a new skill with caution as she navigates her way through the difficulties.

◥ **INTO YOUR ARMS**
A sandy beach provides a safe, open space in which a child can practice walking. Some of the best shots you can take of these early strides are with the toddler heading directly towards you as you shout words of encouragement.

▶ GOING SHOPPING
Don't be afraid to frame the child loosely when he or she is in an open space. This shot shows the independence that children get when they can make their own way around, as the adults are just out of view.

▼ KEEP YOUR DISTANCE
Once the child has developed some confidence at walking, you should shoot from further away — allowing the child to explore without you getting in the way. Such shots make for interesting sequences.

◤ STANDING START
Before children learn to walk, they must first learn how to stand on their own two feet. You can see the concentration on this boy's face as he tries to remain upright.

Food, glorious food!

It might be tempting only to photograph children when they are pretty and photogenic, but to do so means missing some of their most enjoyable moments. Eating is one of those everyday things that you might not think to photograph. But although you might resist showing people with their mouths filled with food, and with their faces covered in chocolate, such shots do have their own charm.

There is also a progression in a child's eating skills. The move from milk to solids is an important milestone, as are the first adventures with finger foods. Along the route to mastering the knife and fork, there will be many a delightful mucky face. There is also the advantage with such shots that young children are usually at their most restful when they have a favourite meal or snack in front of them.

▲ ALL DRESSED UP
Oversized portions of food can help make great pictures — whether a slice of watermelon or a icecream sundae. Both look out of scale when held by a young child. Here ,the boy tackles his giant dessert with obvious apprehension, as he worries about ruining his best clothes.

▶ FIRST MEAL OF THE DAY
Food eaten outdoors gives the photographer more scope for pictures, as there is a more varied choice of background, and better natural light. This picture tells a simple story — the young boy waits impatiently for his older brother to finish his cornflakes so that they can play together.

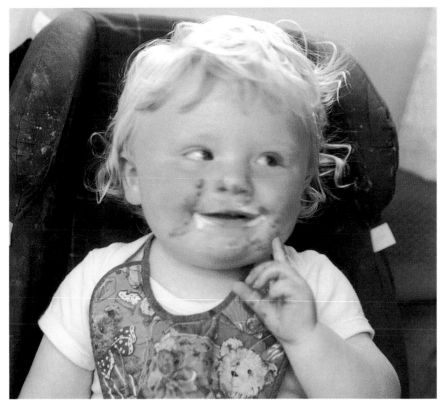

▲ CHEEKY!
Despite the tell-tale signs of a messily eaten ice-cream all over his face, this precocious little boy wags his finger as if to reprimand his parents.

▼ I WANT MORE
A meal time with a child is always full of little incidents — things that make an interesting sequences for the family album. Here the baby happily drinks the bottle of milk, and when it is finished waves it at the mother to show that she wants some more.

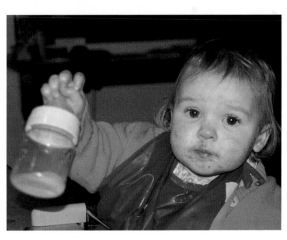

KEEPING CLEAN

A mucky face will look fun in the occasional picture, but you don't want every shot like this.

One of the most useful accessories for shots of babies and young children is a damp flannel!

Dressing up

By the age of two or three, children will not only be developing their own likes and dislikes, but they can communicate these to you more effectively. At this age, the photographer has far more control over how cooperative the child is going to be. If the picture session is tedious, the child will tell you and take appropriate action. One way of getting children on your side is to get them involved in the picture-taking process. This might mean asking them simply to pose with a toy of their choice. A more adventurous plan is to get them to dress up as favourite characters. They might have dressing-up clothes of their own, or you may borrow or hire some. By getting involved in helping them make their choices, and suggesting ways to make the transformation better — with face paint, perhaps, or jewellery — you will win the child's trust. The shoot then becomes an enjoyable game for both of you.

◀ **LAUREN POSING**
A front doorstep makes a simple makeshift studio for a sequence of dressing-up photographs. The white walls around the door frame act as reflectors, helping to ensuring soft, even lighting.

◄ PRETTY IN PINK
So that the young girl filled the natural frame of the doorway better, I got her to stand on a wooden box.

► YOUNG PRINCESS
Small changes can help the subject blend into the surroundings better. For this shot I laid a duvet cover over the box, which toned nicely with the girl's rich purple dress.

◄ LITTLE MERMAID
Get the child to play the part as well as dress the part. The diving pose in this shot helps to convey that she has dressed up as a mermaid. The blue cloth over the box not only tones with her skirt, but also reminds us of the colour of the ocean.

► CACKLING WITCH
A sniggering facial expression and contorted hands help to strengthen the great witch costume. On this occasion the box was covered with black bin bags so that it matched the colour of the girl's cape and pointed hat.

Hat tricks

Whilst full fancy dress is great fun in photographs, it is not necessary to go to all this expense and effort. Often a simple accessory is all that you need to transform a way a child looks. Of all the possibilities, hats are undoubtedly the most versatile.

The great advantage of headgear is not just that it provides excitement to proceedings, it also has a useful part to play in the composition. A hat creates a distinctive border between the face of the child you are photographing and the background. With little effort, a distracting backdrop is distanced or even hidden.

Hats come in all different styles and sizes, and this can be used to provide a strong graphical shape to the picture. The colour of the headgear can also be used to create impact, or to tone with other hues in the composition.

Other accessories that you might successfully use in your picture, and that children will enjoy playing with, include headscarves, tiaras, umbrellas, parasols and sunglasses.

◁ FRAMED
Some hats create a frame within the frame (see page 80), which then neatly isolates the face from the rest of the picture.

▶ MATCHING CURVES
Hats can be used to match existing colours in the scene. Here, the girl's hat not only matches the colour of the tent, it also mimics its curved shape

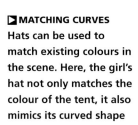

◁ BONNET PARADE
Hats are essential wear for babies of all ages, keeping the sun off their sensitive skin or keeping their heads from getting cold. A wide variety of different styles is available commercially.

◀ **CHANGING FACES**
This unusual hat changes the shape of the face of this girl.

▼ **CONEHEAD**
This pretty bonnet successfully ensures that the girl's head is isolated from the background.

▲ **IN THE SHADE**
Hats, of course, tend to throw the features into shade, so if they have a large brim you may need to use a sheet of white card or a newspaper to reflect light back into the face.

▲ **RIOT OF COLOUR**
A red hat in this picture adds to the riot of colour that is already in the scene!

By the seaside

First visits to the sea are joyous occasions for a toddler. Water and sand may not be new to them, but seeing them in such quantities will be a powerful new experience. Then there are the simple pleasures of digging, without anyone worrying about the mess, and the waves to jump and splash around in.

The trouble is that salt water and fine sand are not good companions for the camera. Even if you are are very careful, it is all too easy for spray and dust to find their way into the delicate electronics and mechanics inside your camera.

You can protect your camera with a clear plastic bag wrapped round the camera; you will still be able to take pictures, but kicked sand won't prove a disaster. If you spend a lot of time on or by the water, special waterproof housings can be bought for most cameras. A cheaper alternative is a disposable camera, which comes pre-loaded with film, and which once used is handed over in its entirety to the processing lab.

▶ SAND EVERYWHERE
Visits to seaside are full of ritual. Here, the little boy learns that you should to wash the sand from your feet when you come back from the beach.

▶ CASTLE BUILDING
Young children can amuse themselves for hours digging in the sand, carrying water from the sea, and collecting pebbles and shells that they find on the beach. Their distraction means that you can shoot pictures without them being aware of the camera.

▲ LOST IN THE ROCKS
On a crowded beach, you will want to zoom in close to ensure that only the people you know are in shot. But when possible, wider framing is useful. The size of the sea, the expanse of sand, and the huge rocks will all be emphasised with the inclusion of a single small child.

▶ COLOUR POWER
Some colours leap out at you in photographs, whilst others seem to recede into the distance. Combine the two, and you create a picture that looks more three-dimensional than usual. In this shot, the red clothes, hat and bucket dominate the composition, whilst the blue sky, reflected off the wet sand, fades away in the background.

READY FOR ALL WEATHERS

Some compact cameras are sold as being 'weatherproof' or 'splashproof" This means they offer limited protection against water and sand — but it does not mean that they can be submerged in the sea! However, such cameras are excellent for those who lead an outdoor lifestyle — or are accident-prone.

◀ RUGGED COMPANION
Unlike normal cameras, weatherproof have seals that are designed to stop water and dust penetrating their casing. But this does not mean they are fully waterproof.

Special occasions

▶ **READY FOR CHURCH**
It is nice to mark special occasions with portraits that take advantage of everyone being in their best clothes. This shot of mother and child would be a perfect memento of the christening day.

For many people, cameras only ever come out on high days and holidays. But even if you are taking regular pictures of the newest additions to the family, there are still some occasions that you absolutely must capture on film. A baby's first birthday, for instance, will be an event of which you will want to make sure that you get good pictures.

The other red-letter days in your baby's first few years will probably depend greatly on the customs and religious festivals that your family holds dear. For some, this might include the child's christening or baptism. Then there are key

▲ **ALL THE FAMILY**
Family gatherings on special occasions like Christmas allow you to shoot group portraits which may not usually be possible. Elderly relatives will love being given special shots of them with their young relations, whilst the babies will cherish these shots in years to come.

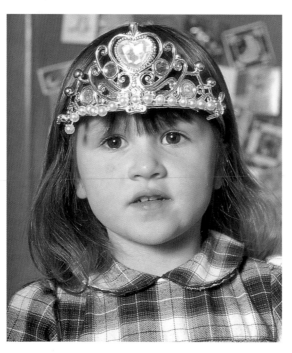

◀ **BIRTHDAY GIRL**
A young girl on her third birthday. Here, the shot is cropped tight to mask the party going on all around. The birthday cards on the wall make a fitting out-of-focus backdrop, whilst the birthday girl is only too happy to wear her newly- acquired tiara.

▲ **BIRTHDAY BANQUET**
Kids' birthday parties are not neat,orderly affairs, and wide-angle shots can tend to look messy. If you want a shot of the spread, take the shot before everyone starts eating!. Here, I stood on a chair to get a high enough vantage point.

▶ SET-UP SHOTS

Don't be afraid to set up shots specially to mark a particular occasion. After this boy's party I arranged the cake and some presents against a plain backdrop, and asked the boy to blow out the candles. The action, away from the pressure of the party, can be repeated several times, so that you end up with a shot that everyone is happy with.

PRINTING YOUR OWN CARDS

Rather than buying commercially made greetings cards, you can make your own using some of your favourite, or most fitting, pictures of your children.

Digital images that have been scanned into your computer or downloaded from a digital camera can be easily designed into cards. Basic word-processing or desktop-publishing software will allow you to import pictures into your card design, though it is possible to buy special greeting-card programs.

If you don't have a digital camera or scanner, most processing laboratories are able to put your pictures onto CD for you, at the time of processing or later.

A family Christmas card could be set up in advance with your new baby dressed as Santa, or surrounded by presents. Birth announcement cards could be printed out with one of your favourite shots of the new arrival in the family.

Print your designs on special card which can be bought to work with standard ink-jet printers. The thicker the card, the better, but choose a type that is double-sided, so that you can print or write a greeting inside.

If you don't have a computer, you can always have multiple copies of the same print made, and then stick these onto card yourself.

◀ SPECIAL GREETINGS
This shot would make a card that all your relatives will cherish.

◄ **UNEXPECTED MOMENTS**
Even set-up shots can produce impromptu moments. In this sequence, it was the boy who decided to take hold of the candles, rather than to blow them out on the cake in a more traditional manner. In this frame, I like the way that he has screwed up his eyes because of the smoke from the candles.

festivals, such as Christmas, Thanksgiving, Diwali, New Year or Passover.

In the first year or so, such festivities will have little meaning to the babies themselves. A birthday party may well be thrown to celebrate the end of the child's first year, but it will be the adults that enjoy the get-together most. And it will be the same for other early celebrations. It is only from the age of two that children will be able to begin to enter into the spirit of such occasions. But even from the baby's birth these

events produce great picture opportunities, simply because they are times when the whole family traditionally comes together. These are the occasions that uncles, aunts, cousins and great-grandparents can be photographed with the new member of the clan.

The pomp of such occasions normally also means that everyone is dressed at their best, rooms are specially decorated to create colourful backgrounds, and that everyone has time on their hands to cooperate with your picture ideas.

Candid camera

ASKING PERMISSION

Some people are sensitive about having their picture taken, and may be even more concerned about pictures being taken of their children.

It is usually best to ask for permission from a guardian whenever possible, so that you avoid any misunderstanding or objection.

If you don't speak the language, you can get the message across by pointing the camera then to the child. Smile, be polite, and never pester.

Often it is worth taking a picture quickly, then asking permission, otherwise the shot is lost.

A small gift may be appropriate in some countries, as a way to show your gratitude. Local guides should be able to advise on this.

The arrival of a baby in the family is often the catalyst for someone to get interested in photography for the very first time, or after a break of many years. Once you have been bitten by the bug, you will want to explore other subjects — landscapes, architecture, sport, wildlife and so on. But you will find yourself returning to child photography, even when your own brood has grown up and left the nest.

When travelling, in particular, you will find that pictures of the local people will help bring colour and life to your portrayal of a new location. Your shots of splendid cathedrals,

▶ **LUNCHTIME!**
The juxtaposition between this huge bowl of fruit and the charming-looking baby couldn't fail to produce a good photograph.

▶ **ROOM TO MANOEUVRE**
So that you do not intrude into people's personal space, a lens with a focal length of 200mm or more is ideal for candid shots. You can get away with less telephoto settings, and in a crowd it is even possible to shoot close-ups of people with a wide-angle lens, without them being aware that you are pointing the camera at them.

Most parents soon
discover that a good
feed is the easiest way
to get their baby or
toddler to bed, but not
many of us use a fishing
boat for a cot!

ancient castles and majestic mountains might be
stunning, but there is always a special attraction
in taking photographs of the woman selling fruit
in the local market, or the old men huddled
together at the street corner. But the local
children can have a particular attraction when it
comes to candid photography.

It's not just the obvious cuteness that young
children have. The problem with photographing
strangers is whether or not to disturb them and
enter their space. Unless you have a very long
lens, it is often hard to photograph strangers
without them knowing what you are doing. It's
not a matter of embarrassment — once someone
has seen the camera, their behaviour is likely to
change, and the picture you saw is lost for ever.
Children, however, are generally not as shy and
reserved as adults. They are happy to show their
emotions in public, and will carry on in their own
egocentric world even when you've been
spotted. Their games, clothes and expressions
make perfect subjects for your camera, showing
you things about the life and customs of a
country that shots of the normal tourist sites
never can.

▶**BUSY BEE**
Carnivals, processions
and other local
festivities are well
worth making a special
effort to visit when on
one's travels. These
events provide a chance
to see people at their
most colourful.

◀**COVERED IN SPOTS**
Another glorious
costume spotted at a
carnival. Participants at
such events expect to be
photographed, so it is
not essential to ask
permission. However, by
asking nicely, you might
get the performers to
hold a particular pose, or
smile in your direction.

▲ BORN PERFORMER
Just because a child plays to the camera does not mean that you are unlikely to get interesting pictures. The pretend hat and the wide-eyed expression make this shot.

▶ ON THE LOOK-OUT
Often children in other parts of the world are as fascinated by you as you are by them. The painted pattern on the side of this building already creates an interesting scene, and the peeking girl provides the finishing touch.